The
Citizens Initiative Party

Other books by Richard L. Freitag

The Responsible Party

The Citizens Initiative Party

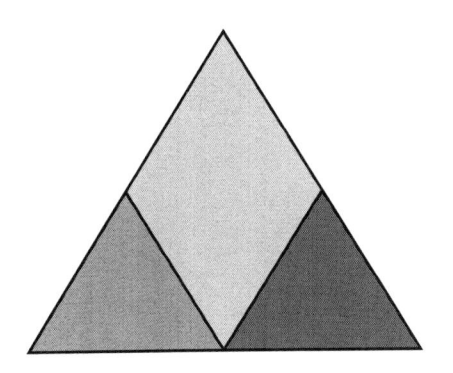

Richard L. Freitag

The Conservative Alternative
Publishing & Distributing Co.
Eau Claire, Wisconsin

The Citizens Initiative Party

Copyright © 2014 by Richard L. Freitag

Published by:
The Conservative Alternative Publishing & Distributing Co.
1416 Cameron Street
Eau Claire, WI 54703-5058
Phone: 715-835-9034 or 715-563-4736
E-mail: rlfdixcorp@charter.net

Published April 2014
All rights reserved

No part of this book may be reproduced or transmitted in any form or by any means without written permission from the author, except in the case of brief quotations embodied in critical articles and reviews.

Ideas in this book were first introduced in *The Responsible Party* by Richard L. Freitag (original edition © 2004 and revised edition © 2007)

ISBN: 978-0-9911609-0-7

Printed in the United States of America

Warning!

Reader, beware! You are reading a call to action for all citizens who are not pleased with "politics as usual" in the United States of America.

I believe the elected members of both of the major political parties have failed to represent the best interests of the constituents who elected them. Furthermore, I believe neither the Republicans nor the Democrats will have the vision, wisdom, willpower, or leadership to alter current policies and entrenched political positions. The result of this disastrous political posturing is our current political stalemate. The failed policies and political ineptitude of these elected Democrats and Republicans, coupled with their aloofness and arrogance toward the voting public, have brought about the sorry state of affairs confronting our nation and our nation's future.

The voting public and, more importantly, our heirs will be forced to find painful solutions to repair the damage done by those who have been elected to positions of national responsibility yet who accept no responsibility for their collective incompetence. This is pure MBE (male bovine excrement)!

The purpose of this book is to create a discussion among concerned American citizens who care about America's future. It seems clear the elected members of the two existing major political parties are not at all concerned about our nation's tomorrow.

This book is an offering of ideas for a restructured political framework. The intent is not to create more rhetoric (we already have enough of that), but rather to stimulate discussion and action to create ***a third, new, major, permanent political party.*** The hope is to salvage the America we love from the present tragedy created by elected members of the two existing major parties.

I believe positive change for this nation can only be accomplished by inspired citizens who are willing and capable of taking the initiative to form a third party.

Time is of the essence.

Table of Contents

Preface ix

I.	Introduction	1
II.	Baggage	11
III.	Observations	39
IV.	Triangulation	46
V.	Looking Back	50
VI.	Looking Ahead	63
VII.	Stagecoach	69
VIII.	Beautiful Garden	77
IX.	Magicians	94
X.	Untouchables	100
XI.	Political Correctness	107
XII.	Alternative Caricature Ideas	117
XIII.	Public Education Lesson	121
XIV.	Formation, Objectives, and Organization of the Party	134
XV.	Operations and Policies of the Party	143
XVI.	Membership in the Party	151

XVII.	Political Platform of the Citizens Initiative Party	158
XVIII.	Other Considerations	166
XIX.	The Future and Your Choices	171
XX.	Addendum	178
	The Constitution of the United States	180
	Constitutional Amendments	202
	The Declaration of Independence	219

Preface

About 2,500 years ago in ancient Greece (the birthplace of democracy and representative government), there lived a great military and political leader — a marvelous statesman, charismatic orator, and politician by the name of Pericles (495 B.C. to 429 B.C.). So popular was Pericles that he was acclaimed "the first citizen of Athens."

For twenty-nine years, Pericles was elected *Strategos* (general and leader) of the city/state of Athens. During his rule, the Acropolis and the Parthenon were constructed. It was said of Pericles that "he kept himself untainted by corruption."

There are a number of quotations and thoughts attributed to Pericles which, in our present times and given our present political situation, are well worth review and contemplation, even though these thoughts originated so long ago.

I believe the following selected quotations and thoughts of Pericles are fitting for your consideration:

"What you leave behind is not what is engraved in stone monuments, but what is woven into the lives of others."

"Freedom is the sure possession of those alone who have the courage to defend it."

"We do not say that a man who takes no interest in politics is a man who minds his own business; we say he has no business here at all."

"Just because you do not take an interest in politics doesn't mean politics won't take an interest in you."

Based on my readings, Pericles viewed people who lived in ancient Athens as falling into three basic categories:

1. *Aliens* — foreigners who lived in the city/state.

2. *Residents* — people who lived in the area but had no political involvement.

3. *Citizens* — people who had Athenian parentage and who were politically involved in the affairs of the public.

The ideas I express in this book were originally formed more than two decades ago. Presenting these concepts for your consideration began as a way of venting my frustration with what I believed to be the ongoing political ineptitude at all levels of government. Over time, it has become obvious that merely griping, being critical, and complaining about the obvious problems within our government effects no change for the better. Understanding that criticism alone achieves nothing other than the opportunity to personally vent, I decided to offer a number of thoughts and ideas for making improvements and positive changes within government or, at the very least, alternatives to "government as usual."

It is my long-held belief that finding fault, complaining, or simply being critical takes little thinking at all. Criticism is nothing more than observation followed by a reporting of what is felt to be wrong, lacking, or at fault. Critics abound, and most seem to be ultimately concerned with projecting an aura of intellectual superiority. While content to point out problems or just whine, few critics offer solutions or alternatives which would require substantially more cerebral effort.

Wouldn't it be wonderful if critics would apply a little of their perceived wisdom and superior mental capacity to offer solutions to the problems they observe? What if critics would become proactive rather than simply dwelling in the pool of negativism they seem to enjoy creating?

Richard L. Freitag

Not content to be just another critic or whiner, I decided it was my desire to try to effect positive change within the current political arena. In an attempt to positively influence a change from our present "government as usual," there would need to be offered at least a few alternatives or potential solutions for a new direction in government. I hope the ideas offered in this book will be considered by you and others who share real concern for our country's future.

In truth, this is my third attempt at this book. It has been published twice before under the title *The Responsible Party*. The theme of both of these previous attempts was that of advocating political moderation. Evidently, most people are not all that interested in being politically moderate, nor are they open to a discussion of responsibility, especially when politics is involved. My political naiveté drove me to believe that there were people who wanted to act in a responsible manner and that there was a political "middle ground" for many that made political sense. At that time, my naiveté caused me to equate moderation with reasonableness, rationality, practicality, and sound judgment. I have since taken a different view. While moderation may at times deliver desired results, this is not always the case, so to rely on moderation as the preferred direction for progress is foolish. Then too, it's difficult to be **passionately moderate**.

The Citizens Initiative Party

In addition, "political responsibility" may be just another oxymoron similar to "good lawyer," "government planning," and "military intelligence."

At any rate, some of the material in this book comes from my past work, which has been embellished or revamped. A great deal of the content of this book is entirely new material derived from a redirected thought process. As the political mess has increased and become more complex over time, it has become necessary for me to rethink many of my past beliefs.

The first two manuscripts for this work were reviewed by a number of friends and even a relative or two. All offered suggestions for improvement, enhancements, corrections, and clarifications to the thoughts and ideas expressed therein. I am most grateful for their continued support.

Generally, authors dedicate their work to their spouses and families, thanking them for their assistance, patience, and understanding during the writing process. So, I should dedicate this book to my wife, Kathryn, who has been there with help, support, and editing for me all the way during this writing.

Instead, it is fitting and proper that this book be dedicated to those American citizens who, like me, believe the time is at hand to form a new, major, permanent, third political party that will be the catalyst for the

Richard L. Freitag

salvation and restoration of the greatness of the United States of America. We are the citizens who believe there can be no reformation of politics or government without that third party, which, though talked about for years, has eluded us for so long.

We no longer believe Democrats or Republicans have the answers to the problems facing this nation. Therefore, citizens like you and me have had enough of the two-party system. We equally deplore both of these parties and their elected officials, who give precedence to the interests of the two parties' agendas, while the best interests of the citizens generally are relegated to that of a secondary consideration or to a mere afterthought, if at all.

So, this book is dedicated to you, my fellow political malcontents. It is we who believe it is time for the citizens of this nation to take the initiative. It is we who believe that only such initiative and such action will make the reformative changes this government needs.

Richard L. Freitag

I. Introduction

One spring evening in the early 1990s, I was watching a nationally broadcast news program when the news anchor shared a brief piece concerning a government study. Initially, this report seemed less than noteworthy. However, contained in this news blurb was an underlying, unreported message — a statement concerning a political and socioeconomic undercurrent at work across this nation.

Despite the fact that more than two decades have passed since that evening, the unreported message in that government study has remained fixed in my mind. This particular government-funded study made it glaringly obvious, at least to me, that a third, permanent, major political party is needed to solve our nation's problems.

This brief and seemingly bland statistical study about the financial makeup of our American society at that time went something like this: *According to a government survey, 15 percent of the U.S. population lives below the poverty line as defined by $15,000 or less of* *annual household income. The report further went on to say that 14 percent of the U.S. population lives above the wealth line as defined by $75,000 or greater annual household income.*

Remember, this survey was from the early 1990s, but the point of the survey is still the same, although the numbers have changed in the two decades since it was reported.

The news anchor moved on to the next news item of the day. I could not.

It was not possible for me to move past that story, because I was transfixed, not by what I had just heard, but rather by the unmentioned implications of the figures cited in the study.

Overwhelmed by the unspoken message contained in the tiny news item I had just heard, my thought process was focused on the political as well as the socioeconomic polarities implicit in that report. That government survey and the findings reported therein have given me cause to consider at great length what was really being said about the political, social, and economic makeup of our society. Additionally, this report pointed out to me how various segments of our society are, or are not, being represented politically.

Where am I headed with all of this?

Consider this. There exists a generally accepted belief

as to which major political party supposedly represents the interests of the population living below the poverty line — the Democratic Party. This is, at least, the claim of the Democratic Party, and many in our society seem to believe this to be a fact. There also exists a commonly held belief about which major political party represents the interests of the population living above the wealth line — the Republican Party. Again, many in our society seem to believe this to be a fact.

So far, so good.

The question then that will not go away for me is this: *Which of these two major political parties represents the interests of the large percent of the population that is neither wealthy nor impoverished but that ends up paying for the excesses of those on either end of the financial spectrum of American society?* In the 1990s report, this middle population was 71 percent.

While both major political parties claim to represent the interests of the 71 percent, there remains the hard truth that the 71 percent — known as the **middle class** — is tasked with funding government expenditures that benefit both the very rich and the very poor. The middle class is carrying this financial burden without the benefit of a dedicated political voice to represent its interests.

It is believed the very poor can't pay their fair share of the fiscal burden, and the very wealthy, who can afford to pay, enjoy tax loopholes and tax avoidance vehicles. So the burden of taxation falls on the middle class.

Both of the major political parties pander to the interests of the 71 percent only because it is necessary to their purposes of *fund raising,* especially during political campaigns before every election. Make no mistake about this. ***Their only goal in pandering to the middle class is to raise money for their party operations and their particular party's political agenda.***

Do not believe for a moment that either of the two major political parties have any interest in the well-being of middle-class Americans. In their view, the middle class exists to be exploited, to be used politically and financially. Our middle-class pockets are pilfered in the sole interest of providing funds for those members of society in either the upper 14 percent or the lower 15 percent of our nation's population. Meanwhile, nothing whatsoever is done for those of us who make up the 71 percent.

No doubt, concerned citizens of any nation with a representative form of government should hold membership in a political party. However, if the political posturing of the two major political parties makes no sense to citizens who wish to find a political "home," who want to be kindred spirits with those who believe as they do, it is difficult, if not impossible, to justify membership in either party. So long as there is no political party wherein middle-class citizens can feel comfortable and justified — feel that the party is a fit for them — how can it be expected that disenfranchised citizens would want to become politically involved? Further, without a politically involved citizenry, how can there truly be a "government of the people, by the people, and for the people"? Presently, it seems, we have a government of, by, and for the politically connected few of the 29 percent at the expense of the 71 percent.

Ask yourself: Do either of the major parties speak to your needs, your core beliefs, your moral or ethical values? Do either of the major parties make it a habit of expressing a point of view you can identify with? Have you tried in vain to convince yourself that one or the other major political party speaks for you and those like you? Can you convince yourself that you and those like you have any real political representation?

Do you believe both of the major political parties have polarized themselves by representing the interests of either the very rich or the very poor or either the ultraconservative or the extreme liberal? Do you agree there definitely exists political polarization?

Do you believe this polarization is a major cause of the political impasse, the gridlock, and the stalemate in our nation's legislative process?

And if this polarization — this "either/or" representation — exists to represent the interests of the 14 percent and the 15 percent, do you continue to question **WHO** is representing you, because you are part of the 71 percent?

Those of us who make up the middle class have no one really looking out for us, speaking on our behalf, or representing our best interests.

If the political posturing of the two existing major political parties continues with their radical "left wing" or "right wing" political positions, those of us who believe that both positions are equally unrealistic, idealistic, nonsensical, unreasonable, and impractical are left politically adrift in a representational chasm. While both parties claim to be the champions of the middle class, the hard truth is that neither party really is that champion *and they do not really care.*

While the middle class deserves representation just as much as the rich and the poor, *do not expect to see that void filled* by candidates of either party in the near or even the distant future. We will not be represented because we are of no political interest to either major party. We don't make "good story." Being middle class isn't the right stuff for good media coverage. Terrible poverty or vast wealth makes for good story lines and, therefore, results in calls for political action by the

The Citizens Initiative Party

media who give cause to outraged citizens. But we of the middle class should be outraged even more so, given our lack of real political representation.

So, just in case you haven't been following along, let me repeat this basic question: ***Which of the two major political parties speaks on your behalf, expresses your best interests, shares your moral point of view, and represents the interests of citizens who are neither rich nor poor?***

You're right! Neither!

The presidential election of 1992 and, to a lesser degree, the 1996 election demonstrated clearly that there are citizens in this nation who are not pleased with the political ineptitude of our government and the political posturing of the major political parties. Mr. H. Ross Perot's 19 percent of the popular vote in the 1992 election demonstrated clearly that nearly 1 in 5 voters were willing to cast their ballots for Perot in a futile attempt to send a message to our elected officials in Washington, D.C.

Among other things, that message expressed an unwillingness of those Perot voters to continue to tolerate major party politicians ignoring 71 percent of the citizenry. Additionally, those voters declared an unwillingness to accept the continued hypocrisy of the major political parties where the middle class is concerned.

Our vote said we were no longer interested in the arrogant usury, disregard, and even contempt for the political interests of middle-class Americans.

Many of us who voted for Mr. Perot back in 1992 and again in 1996 are proud of the ballot we cast for him and his ideas. We voted for Mr. Perot because we wanted to, tried to, felt a need to send a wake-up call to Washington, D.C. That wake-up call definitely went unheard.

So, what to do?

Those of us who are not happy with the politics of the major political parties can continue to complain and whine as we listen to the ongoing pandering by major political party politicians prior to elections. We can continue to get lost in the smoke screen thrown up by "blame game politics" practiced by both parties. If we should choose to believe what they say, we can be assured we will continue down the same hopeless path of our past. We will continue to be paid lip service by those who supposedly represent our best interests. However, be assured that continued lip service and pandering will effect no political improvement whatsoever for the middle class.

Only proactive involvement in a new, permanent, third major political party can and will effect the positive political change desired by those of us who are not happy with "politics as usual."

The Citizens Initiative Party

Entrenched government and political systems will not and cannot change until and unless new ground is broken. There must be new vision, new philosophy, and a new initiative — a new political direction — to clean up the polarized political mess we face today. We must begin with a fresh page, uncluttered by past political practices and the political hacks of the past who perpetuate entrenched practices. We must form a new, permanent, third, major political party whose elected officials will truly listen to and represent the interests of all of the citizens of this nation, including those of us in the middle class.

The time to take action is now! For those of us wishing to effect positive political change in the United States of America, we need to understand that time is of the essence! The kind of political change we envision can only be effected by organizing, activating, and energizing a new, permanent, third, major political party. This party is not to be just another flash-in-the-pan, one-shot run at the presidency. Rather, this new party needs to be a permanent and, more importantly, significant part of America's political future.

The goal of this book is to get enough concerned citizens to take action — to take the initiative politically. These citizens must work together to form a third party that will become and remain active on the American

Richard L. Freitag

political scene until, like the two existing parties, it too loses its vision and direction or loses touch with the citizens it is supposed to represent.

II. Baggage

Each individual's thought process or philosophy comes with personal baggage. Therefore, I believe I must share some of my background so you can come to understand the how, where, and why of the thoughts and ideas I share with you.

If you prefer to fast-forward past the details of my background, feel free to advance to Chapter III to learn more about the political action I'm proposing.

My intention here is to explain some of the life experiences that are the foundation of my thought process.

Each of us has our own "baggage." You have yours. Here is mine.

I was born June 26, 1950, to a small-time excavating and grading contractor father and a registered nurse mother — definitely middle class all the way. Dad was third-generation American of pure Swiss ancestry. (My last name is directly translated to the day of the week — Friday — from the Germanic Swiss language). Mother is third-generation American of half German and half

Swedish ancestry. I grew up in a smaller, west-central Wisconsin city — Eau Claire (French for clear water), population 35,000 in my youth — and I had a public school education from kindergarten through the twelfth grade in the Eau Claire public school system.

Noteworthy is the fact that I attended first grade and second grade at a traditional one-room country school, with grades one through eight in one large classroom and one teacher for all eight grades.

After the second grade, my family moved into the city, where my exceptional third-grade teacher found me to be illiterate and encouraged my mother to send me to summer school remedial reading classes, which I did attend. When I entered the fourth grade, I could read, thanks to Miss Anderson.

It would be fair to say I was never much of a student. I did very well with those subjects that either challenged me or interested me. I did poorly with those subjects that didn't interest me. I'm not certain I didn't have ADD (attention deficit disorder), but that hadn't been invented back then. When bored, my mind wandered, and I was embarrassed quite often when teachers called upon me in the classroom. With less than stellar grades, I graduated from high school in 1968 with a D final grade in algebra/trigonometry, but I got out the door with a diploma at any rate.

The Citizens Initiative Party

During my school years, ever since the third grade, I was involved in the programs of the Boy Scouts of America — first as a Cub Scout and later as a Boy Scout. I became an Eagle Scout at the age of 16. My Scouting experience has been a profound influence on my life in so many ways.

Unlike many of my classmates, who knew exactly what they wanted to do with their lives after graduation, I was adrift concerning my plans for my future. At least most of my classmates knew for certain that they were not in any way interested in serving or being drafted into the military at that time. As this was the height of the Vietnam War, many elected to go to college. I had dreamed of being a mechanical engineer, but with that D final grade in mathematics, which is the foundation of engineering, I knew I wasn't a prime candidate for engineering school.

As a senior in high school, I had been talking to an Army recruiter for several months prior to graduation. I wanted Army armor — TANKS! I graduated at the age of 17, so three weeks later, on my 18th birthday, I went to the recruiting office to sign up. The recruiter I had been previously dealing with had been transferred, and a new guy was there in his place. Upon entering the office, he greeted me in a friendly manner and asked what he could do for me. I introduced myself.

This new recruiter said, "Oh yes, I have your paperwork right here. You'll be leaving for basic training in three days."

I said, "No, that's not what I had agreed to. I was supposed to leave in September on the delayed enlistment program. That's the deal I had worked out with the other recruiter."

He instantly got ugly and said, "Don't you go telling me what is or is not going to happen; I'll tell you!"

To which I replied, "Tell you what, Sergeant, why don't you stick that paperwork where the light don't shine. No deal."

I had never signed anything up to that point, so I left that office immediately. Now what to do?

I went down to the Navy recruiters office. There was a huge poster on the wall about the U.S. Navy Seabees. I was more than familiar with the Seabees because my Uncle Bob had been one of the original World War II Seabees. So the recruiter and I started to talk. He made it known to me that there was a special recruitment program going on for Seabees and that if recruits could prove they had construction skills or training and could get that training documented, new recruits could enter the Navy with advanced ranks. This sounded good to me.

My dad, the excavating and grading contractor, had

seen to it that I learned about clutching and shifting on farm tractors at the age of eight. At nine, I was on a crawler tractor learning to clutch, shift, steer, and use bucket controls. At 14, I was expected to be able to load trucks with a crawler front-end loader. Over the next couple of years during summer vacation (given my old man, what a joke — vacation!), I learned how to operate a road grader, a bulldozer, and drive heavy trucks. At 16, I was driving trucks with two stick shifts. I learned grading, setting grade, and how to read grade stakes. That summer after graduation, I was reasonably proficient on a number of different construction-site grading machines as well as heavy trucks.

I brought the paperwork home for my dad to fill out to verify that I knew how to operate machinery and trucks.

When I returned the paperwork to the Navy recruiter, he said I would qualify as an Equipment Operator 3rd Class (pay grade E-4 — same as a corporal). Again, this deal sounded good to me. At least as an equipment operator I knew what I would be doing in the Navy. I signed the enlistment papers on the spot.

That September, as my high school friends headed off to college, I left for basic training at the Atlantic Fleet Seabees Headquarters Base at Gulfport, Mississippi. I was 18 years and almost three months old — the youngest recruit in my training company — when I entered active duty. Even though the youngest in the company, I was the only one to score 100 percent on the first-aid test. Because of my Scouting background, first aid was nothing other than a matter of review for me.

After five weeks in Gulfport, I was sent home for one week and then on to the Coronado Naval Amphibious Base at San Diego, California, for about four-and-a-half months. While stationed there, we Seabees were sent to the Camp Pendleton Marine Corps Base for weapons training.

When our orders arrived, my group was sent to the U.S. Naval Support Activity in Da Nang, Vietnam. I was 18 years and nine months old. I served a year in and around the Da Nang area as a heavy truck driver and heavy equipment operator.

During my time there in Vietnam, I turned 19 and studied and passed my examination for Equipment Operator 2nd Class (pay grade E-5 — the same as a sergeant). I was the only one in my outfit to advance in rank. I wanted to prove to myself and the Navy that they hadn't given me an unwarranted gift and that I really was competent. Then too, I think the rank advancement program from my Scouting background came into play once again as a motivating factor. My section Chief Petty Officer figured I was probably the youngest 2nd Class

The Citizens Initiative Party

Petty Officer in the Navy at the time I earned the rank.

I was an honorably discharged Vietnam War veteran, released from active duty at the age of 19 years and nine months old. I had matured a great deal during the time spent in the Navy. My experience had given me very graphic evidence that I needed to further my education. I saw how the Officer Corps lived, compared with how I lived as an enlisted man. I viewed so many of these officers as no different from myself, other than they had a college degree, which I didn't. This is not to sound arrogant, but many of the officers I encountered were lacking in the most basic leadership skills that I had learned in Scouting. But they had that college degree. If a national emergency or war was declared and I had to go back into the military, I wanted that college degree. Living an officer's lifestyle was much more appealing. Since my time in the service qualified me for the G.I. Bill (probably the only government-sponsored program that is a true success story) to help pay for a college education, I decided to pursue a college degree.

I enrolled at the University of Wisconsin-Eau Claire for the 1970 fall semester. In the later years of the 1960s, my local university had developed a School of Business. I chose that course of study because I now knew I wanted to be a part of my dad's business.

Dad had expanded his business during my time in

the service to include landscaping, as well as grading and excavating. He had built a new garden/landscaping retail store during my military absence and, as a result, was heavily in debt. I didn't care much about the landscaping end of the business. But my sister did, and she ran the retail end of the landscaping business. I was far more interested in the earth-moving machinery and the trucking part of the operation.

It was sheer willpower that got me through college. When I feel real generous about my four years at UW-Eau Claire, I speak of two dozen courses that made a positive difference in my life. When feeling less than generous, there are really about twelve courses I believe were worth the time spent. The rest was "fill" for giving me "a well-rounded education."

Like my earlier experience with school, I was no student and only did well in those classes that either made sense to me or that I found to be of interest or in some way worthwhile. In accounting, for example, I learned two things — how to read financial statements and that I *didn't* understand accounting. I knew I'd always have to hire this work done by others. Several business classes were marvelous, taught by superb instructors who created an atmosphere wherein learning was certain to take place. Then there was the rest of the stuff, which I'll just term MBE (male bovine excrement). In my mind, I quit college at least fifty times. But I went back fifty-one times and got my bachelor of science degree in business administration in 1974.

During my college years, I lived with my parents. My university of choice was in my hometown, so my living expenses were kept to a minimum. Besides going to college, I worked for the family firm as a heavy equipment operator, truck driver, crew chief, and salesman. I was learning the family business as I went to business school. After graduation, with a fresh business degree, I was elected president of our family's corporation. (I believe my dad thought it was a joke.)

Going back:

Two years before I graduated from high school, my dad had embarked into a new area of business that didn't mean all that much to me at the time but would now become an opportunity for me after my return from the military. Dad became involved in a business that was just beginning to take off in our area of the country at the time — growing, harvesting, selling, and installing cultured sod. To define cultured sod, it means that vast fields were planted in turf grass, which was harvested as a crop. This product was either sold as a commodity or delivered and installed as lawns for private homes or athletic fields, or for road ditch "flow lines" or erosion control measures or other purposes. It was a unique business opportunity at the time, and my dad was on the cutting edge in our area. For approximately ten years, we had an exclusive business in our area of operation.

Dad was heavily in debt when I returned from Vietnam because he had built the retail landscape store. His equipment fleet was of pretty poor quality, and his hands were tied financially. The bank wouldn't give him any room to upgrade equipment at the time.

One day in the late summer of 1970, I was sent to deliver a truckload of sod with this absolute junk pile of a truck that I didn't even believe was safe to be on the roads. That same day, Dad had gone to Minneapolis, Minnesota, to purchase repair parts for the crane boom part of the truck. (We delivered our palletized sod on trucks equipped with what was referred to as "block bodies," which consisted of a rotating trolley boom with a cable-operated fork lift attached to lower the loaded pallets to the ground.) When he got back that afternoon, he mentioned that the boom truck dealership had repossessed two nearly new, used block trucks less than a year old from a concrete block company that went broke out in Montana. He said how beautiful these trucks were.

Being a young man and aggressive about business and hating the decrepit vehicle I had been forced to drive that day, coupled with my naiveté at the time concerning the family business financial situation, I boldly asked, "Well, how many of these beautiful trucks are you going to buy?"

"None", he said. "I can't."

"Well then, I'm going to buy one, because I can't stand driving this junk anymore," I said, not really knowing how I was going to do what I claimed I was about to do.

We discussed it, arrived at a delivery price I was to be paid by the family firm, and I moved ahead with the deal. A couple of days later, Dad took me to Minneapolis, where I picked the truck I wanted and bought it. At the age of 20, I was in the trucking business and now personally in debt big time, but I felt I was moving ahead and that I could win as a private businessman — an owner-operator in trucking jargon. I was confident I could make my payments and have a safe, reliable, decent-looking vehicle with which to deliver product.

Within three years I had the truck paid for, and a year later I traded it in on a brand new one. The next year I bought another new truck. The sodding business grew, and I paid off my debt on those trucks as well.

A unique business opportunity came in late 1976. Our area of America's Dairy Land experienced a severe drought that summer. The hay crop, upon which the dairy industry relies, was decimated. Hay production was less than half what it should have been, and dairy farmers were having trouble — so much trouble that the federal government stepped in and funded a long-haul hay supply program for area farmers. Independent truckers would be utilized to transport the hay into our area from distant sources. I wanted to be one of those long-haul truckers.

One of my best friends from my days in the Navy lived in central Kansas. I called John and asked him if there was hay available in his area. He said he'd check. After checking, John called back in a day and invited me to come down. Dad and I made the trip together. John introduced me to farmers, and we made our initial purchases of hay. I had bought the product; now I needed a way to move it.

I attended an auction sale in South Sioux City, Nebraska, where I bought a 1975 Mack truck tractor that was one year old. I bought a new flatbed trailer, and I was in business. I ran hard — harder than a sane man should have. I ran this business, as well as my other businesses over time, in a straight-forward manner, keeping meticulous records and running it by the rules.

At this time there were a number of my competitors who, it seems, just couldn't keep from cheating. Some of these guys bought what they called hay (actually it was bailed swamp grass and tag alders from Northern Minnesota swamps) roughly 150 miles from our area and falsified the records to indicate that this material came from Montana or Colorado or Kansas, or anyplace but from where they actually got the stuff. Since the government was reimbursing the farmers for the transportation costs on a mileage basis, the cheaters were pocketing all kinds of money without incurring the costs associated with the length of travel they were claiming. It was atrocious. Not only was there cheating on the mileage, but more importantly, there was little nutritional value for the cattle in this garbage product that was delivered to the farmers. I was never interested in these sorts of business practices for any reason.

My policy was to always have my loads weighed and ticketed at the nearest grain elevator in either Kansas or Nebraska, where I obtained my hay. I always hauled nothing other than pure alfalfa hay, which was complete nourishment to the livestock I was helping to keep alive and productive. I had customers on a waiting list because it was known that I was running an honest operation.

Besides, I knew that if the government ever wanted to verify or audit my operation or that of my farmer customers, they could go ahead. I had nothing to hide. Not so for the less-than-honest truckers. That was well and good as far as I was concerned, because I have never cared for cheating or cheaters. All you really had to do to be successful in this long-haul hay business (as well as any other business) was to run hard and run honest.

I did both of those things, and I made a great return on my investment, which turned out to be great timing.

That Christmas of 1976, I was engaged to my wife, Kathryn, whom I had met on a blind date during college. My best friend and her best friend were dating and introduced the two of us. Kathy had been teaching school, and I had been long-distance dating her for the past three years when we decided we should marry. So, much of the profits from the long-haul trucking business were used to make a substantial down payment on a brand new, split-level ranch home on the west side of Eau Claire. This is still our home to this day.

We were married on July 16, 1977.

I sold the Mack and the trailer that summer with the same auction company I had bought it through the previous fall. I remained in the sod trucking business with my two boom trucks.

The annual business cycle of big crews in the spring and fall seasons, with a lull in business activity and reduced crew size during the midsummer months, continued as usual for the first three years of our marriage.

Things changed dramatically on the evening before our third anniversary, July 15, 1980, when all hell broke loose in western Wisconsin. Our area of the state was hit with a 100-plus mile-per-hour shear force windstorm that lasted for roughly five hours, causing extensive property damage through the storm path. On the following morning, my parents were scheduled to leave on a trip to France to visit the French foreign exchange student who had lived with the family when I was in Vietnam and her husband. Dad was a one-dimensional workaholic for whom twelve-hour to sixteen-hour days were the norm during our seasonal business activity. The old man saw the extensive business possibilities that lay ahead in light of this natural disaster. My mother had to nearly physically drag my dad to the airport.

No sooner had they left town than the phone rang with a call from the City of Eau Claire Public Works Department mobilizing all of our equipment and trucks, as well as the trucks and equipment of every other contractor in town. The cleanup efforts would go on for over a month, with downed trees blocking streets and with damaged buildings that were smashed up and needing to be hauled off to make way for reconstruction.

We were instantly back in business and on a scale I had never experienced. We went from five employees to seventy-five in a couple of days. Not only did we mobilize all of the equipment we owned, we rented a number of other pieces of machinery as needed. We and all of the other area contractors were working seven days per week during all daylight hours just to get the city opened up for emergency vehicles and general traffic.

Richard L. Freitag

There were power outages in the entire area for well over one week. We had chain saw crews removing trees from buildings, front-end loader and truck crews opening up streets, labor crews demolishing or salvaging buildings, and on and on.

For my sister and me, along with a couple of supervisors, it was a project coordination nightmare. We were working on crew scheduling past midnight many nights just to keep everything and everybody productive. But it worked out well.

When my parents returned from Europe, we had a substantial pile of cash in the bank such as we had never had before. I think this is the first time my dad believed his children had not been dropped head first on the birthing room floor. When he wanted to take over operations upon his return, my sister and I asked him to stay out of our way since we knew how we had things set up and wanted to continue with our routine uninterrupted. The old man hated this, but had the wisdom to know we were right because we had established relationships dealing with clients we had developed in his absence.

We were still heavily involved in the cleanup efforts in our community when neighbors near our place of business decided they wanted to have a nine-hole golf course built on their farm. Dad had built a golf course back in the early 1970s, and he was excited to get at this one. He loved golf course building. He often spoke of the work as "earth sculpting" — more or less an art form.

After meeting with the neighbors and the golf course designer to work out pricing, Dad took a few operators and a few pieces of heavy earth-moving equipment and began transforming a cornfield into a golf course. This was perfect timing, because this project kept him out of my sister's hair and mine.

At this time, a local developer we had done a lot of work for in the past was bidding on a fifteen-unit, low-income housing development in our community to be paid for by the U.S. Department of Housing and Urban Development (HUD). The developer asked me to bid on the excavation and backfill for the basements, the site grading, lawn work, and landscaping. Being an aggressive young businessman, I bid the project even though we were working beyond what we could normally handle at the time. I'll never forget the day I was informed by the developer that they won the project and we got the portion of the work that I had bid. I was excited. I can still remember the old man's comment, "Isn't that just great! We really can't handle what we have going on now and you go land a big one! Now what the hell are we supposed to do?"

The cleanup efforts were slowing down about the time we were to begin the site work and basement excavation for the HUD project. We were able to excavate and backfill the foundations that fall before freeze-up, but the lawn and landscaping work would be a holdover into the 1980 season.

Meanwhile, Dad and his increased golf course construction crew were determined to finish the golf course before winter. The final seeding of the golf course took place December 22 on a day when temperatures hovered around 10 degrees. This was the end of our 1980 season.

As the spring of 1981 began, thankfully we had the HUD project work from the previous fall to finish. Oh yes, we had some sales that spring, but nothing like years past. I have no idea how he did it, but my dad correctly predicted terrible times for our business for not only the 1981 season, but also for the future.

Things were very slow all season. When Dad got a call out of the blue to look at some oil field site work in Williston, North Dakota, he jumped at the chance. He and I went to the oil fields together to look things over. We decided against getting into that business, but we certainly had plenty of "windshield time" to talk things over. I remember him saying, "You will not believe what I am about to tell you, because for this past decade our business has been growing, with the exception of only the current downturn this year. But there will come a time when you and the crew show up at the shop, you open the garage doors to look at the lineup of trucks and equipment, and there will be absolutely nothing to do, no work to be had at any price. There simply won't be anything to do. I've been through this when I was younger. Next year will be bad!"

Toward the end of the 1981 season, we got a major lawn and landscape project around a large manufacturing plant, and we completed it in October.

Dad wasn't feeling well. He saw a doctor, who determined he had colon cancer. His surgery was in mid-November. The colon cancer surgery was successful, and Dad was ready to leave the hospital. My mother was in his room with his change of clothing to wear home when he said that he would rather go back to bed than go home right then. What had happened was that his gall bladder had burst and had internally poisoned his body. He was rushed to surgery. His primary physician was out of town at the time, and Dad, during the surgery to clean the poisons out of his abdominal cavity, went into cardiac arrest. He was basically reduced to a remnant of what he once had been, with only his heart, lungs, and brain stem still functioning. My mother, my sister, and I had to make the decision to turn off the life support machines two days before Thanksgiving. That decision was not a difficult one to make, in spite of what we knew the outcome of that decision would be.

Richard L. Freitag

Mother, my sister, my wife, and I ate our 1981 Thanksgiving Day Feast in the hospital cafeteria that noon. That afternoon Dad died. His funeral was four days later. He was 67 years old. I was amazed at the size of the gathering for his wake and the funeral service that followed. He had been an area businessman for the past forty-plus years. I knew that, but I didn't realize how well-known he had become over all those years.

After my father's passing, I became the chief executive officer (CEO) and chief operating officer (COO) of our family's firm. Although I had been elected CEO back in 1974 after graduation from college, the truth was that my dad never gave up as the top dog — chief operating officer of his firm. That is to say I was CEO in name only back then and up until Dad's passing. But now, all of that changed. I was suddenly thrust into both the executive and operations positions in the company because there simply was no one else to take over. I was 31 years old at the time and wished I had had more time to be mentored and tutored by the old man. All I could do was move the company ahead as best as I knew how with the knowledge and experience I had acquired while working with Dad. Of course, the timing really couldn't have been worse.

Again, how Dad had been able to tell that the 1982 season was going to be so terrible, I have no idea. But the

The Citizens Initiative Party

year was as bad as he had envisioned and worse. We had some holdover contract work for our services on building projects that were not yet completed late the previous season. We were able to maintain the momentum of the previous season until mid-June, when every phase of our business activity suddenly dried up. There was nowhere to go to find projects, and there was absolutely nothing coming up in the future. The outlook was bleak. Although Dad had warned me of this potential situation, I couldn't believe it was possible that things could get this bad. There was nothing to do and nowhere to look for a solution to change the situation.

Over that 1981-82 winter season, home loan interest rates had skyrocketed to unheard-of levels in the range of 21 percent, which crippled the housing industry — the industry we had relied on for so many years for our livelihood. Commercial work was nonexistent as well. I was in contact with everybody I knew in the building industry, only to find they were suffering as badly, if not worse, than we were at the time.

An old armed services buddy from Houston, Texas, called me to let me know he had a project in Oklahoma City, Oklahoma, and he wondered if I wanted to be involved. I would do anything to keep employees employed, so I sent a driver and our largest dump truck to work on a project nearly 1,000 miles from home.

Another seemingly goofy thing happened that year. Our neighbors, who had hired Dad to build a nine-hole golf course, were starving to death under their debt load and the recently heightened interest rates. They asked if we would be willing to build and finance the cost of adding another nine holes to their golf course so that they could increase play and thereby increase revenue to keep the bank off their back. Could we help them with this? Anything just to keep operations going?

We did build and finance the back nine of their golf course. I did the work to keep loyal, long-time employees employed. Was this smart? Probably not!

Our business during 1982-85 could best be summed up as "limping through" the economic downturn we were experiencing as a nation.

Along with the business in a tail spin, another, but positive, major change occurred in my personal life. This had to do with Scouts. An announcement was made regarding my church's Scout troop. Unless a new Scoutmaster was found for Troop 30, the church would drop the troop's charter and the troop would disband. This was my old Boy Scout troop where I had earned my Eagle Scout Award. In addition, the troop was the second oldest one in town, so I wasn't going to let it just fold up. I volunteered to be the Scoutmaster of Troop 30 — a position I held for the next twenty years. I started with five Scouts, dropped to three, and then, with the help of a dedicated group of parents and volunteers, began to build it up. For the final nine years of my career as Scoutmaster, Troop 30 carried a roster of forty to fifty-five Scouts. During my tenure, Troop 30 awarded Eagle Scout awards to fifty-six young men.

I was a strict disciplinarian and tolerated no slackers. No one got a free ride. I constantly raised the bar, never allowing my Scouts to become lethargic. I found that youngsters will always rise to the level of expectation set for them by adult leaders. I always set the bar very high, and I won't apologize for doing that. I know I was considered to be a hard-ass by many other adult leaders in the ten-county area served by the Chippewa Valley Council. I'll gladly accept that criticism. I'm a results guy. Because of my being more interested in results than excuses, numerous young men got to hear my favorite quote from Henry Ford: "Whether you believe you can do a thing or not, you are right." I can't stand excuses, and I loathe excuse makers. A lot of young men came to understand this concept in short order.

Despite this, many of these fine young men still stay in touch with their old Scoutmaster. I've been invited to their graduations, military ceremonies, and weddings. That is the payoff for having been a little more demanding and a lot stricter than some of my peers. Yes, sir, I'll take that criticism for being a little tougher!

I would go so far as to say that my time spent as the Scoutmaster of Troop 30 was, without doubt, the most important, the most rewarding, the most fulfilling, the most worthwhile thing I have ever done with my life! I have received numerous awards and recognitions from the Boy Scouts of America, including being recognized as one of the top sixty-four Scoutmasters in the nation from among the organization's 46,000 Scoutmasters in 1993. But the most rewarding aspect of being involved in Scouting was the positive impact I believe I made on young men's lives. I believe that being a Boy Scout Troop Scoutmaster is my life's greatest achievement!

Now, back to the business ….

With bleak prospects for the 1986 construction season, in mid-January I traveled to Marquette, Michigan, to bid on a nine-hole golf course expansion project at the K.I. Sawyer Air Force Base. On my way to the bid letting, I stopped in Park Falls, Wisconsin. Here I bought a brand new fishing rod with a new Penn Reel at the St. Croix Fishing Rod factory outlet store. I figured that if I didn't win the bid on this golf course project, I may as well spend the summer fishing instead of trying to continue on in a business that was not profitable.

In 1986, I never wet the line on the fishing equipment. Not only did I win the bid for the project at the

The Citizens Initiative Party

K.I. Sawyer Air Force Base, but I also won a project for a nine-hole addition with a remodel of three existing holes at Eagle River, Wisconsin. Later that same season, I won a project in Waukesha, Wisconsin.

For the next fifteen years, I concentrated on golf course construction, building thirty-seven various golf course projects. These projects ranged from smaller remodel jobs to eighteen-hole championship-level projects in four Upper Midwestern states.

I had planned to retire as a golf course construction contractor. That never happened. As an industry during the 1980s and 1990s, we built ourselves out of a job. Nationally, too many golf courses had been constructed, while at the same time there was really no increase in the number of golfers to play the game. This situation of oversupply of available courses for the golfing public resulted in a basic greens fees price war among golf courses.

Golf construction virtually died off. I had a passion for golf construction, and when it died, so did my desire to continue on in business. Although I had expertise in excavation, grading, and landscaping, all these markets were crowded. With hungry competitors "killing one another off" with what I felt to be unrealistically low, cheap pricing, I decided to sell off my trucks and machinery and simply quit business. I found employment for my dedicated employees with other area contractors.

I worked for a couple of seasons as an employee. I operated heavy equipment and drove trucks for a contractor friend of mine, only to find that I enjoyed being an *employer* more than I enjoyed being an *employee*. I worked for the federal government for one summer, so I know and understand the difference between the private and the public sector. WOW, do I ever!

Through what you have just read, I hope you have learned several things about me that affect my outlook and position and opinions on a whole range of topics.

To highlight:

- ▶ I am a former small businessman. I believe in capitalism and free-market enterprise, because I believe it has produced the greatest amount of good for the greatest number of people.
- ▶ I am a construction man. At the end of every day, construction and trades people can look back over their shoulder and see exactly what has been accomplished. Accomplishments are pure and clean and genuine. Work is either done or it's not done. There is no gray area about construction, and I like that. One other neat thing about construction is this: You can talk about being an equipment operator or plumber or electrician; you can read books about any of it; you can

even write about it, but until and unless you have actually accomplished work of some sort or another, you are nothing other than a mouthpiece, a dreamer, or a phony. Only reality counts with construction people. It's pure, and it's simple.
- I am a U.S. Navy Seabees Veteran of the Vietnam War, and I am extremely proud of my service to my country.
- I was the Scoutmaster of Troop 30 for nearly twenty years, and I remain active in troop leadership. The Boy Scouts of America has been a huge influence in my life. I have a fifty-year veteran's pin.
- I'm a results guy — not interested in excuses, only results.
- I have done a lot of volunteer work for a number of different organizations, and I am proud to have done so.
- I am practical and reality-based. I'm no dreamer. This is a result of my experience as a businessman.
- I am a married man of thirty-six years.
- I am a longtime member of the following organizations: Chippewa Valley Council–Boy Scouts of America, Vietnam Era Seabees, American Legion Post 413, Sunrise Exchange Club of Eau Claire, and Eau Claire Curling Club.

Richard L. Freitag

▶ I am a *life member* of the following organizations: My church, Veterans of Foreign Wars Post 305, Vietnam Veterans of America Chapter 5, the National Lutheran Association of Scouters, and the National Eagle Scout Association.

All of these life experiences are my background and are the factors that influence my decisions, my outlook, my opinions, and my biases.

I share all of this with you not to boast, not to brag, but rather just so you will know these basic things about me and my past. It is only right that you know.

Now you have a brief glimpse into my "baggage."

III. Observations

For your consideration, this will be a review of some of the good and some of the not so good within our government and our current political environment.

It is essential that all concerned citizens of the United States of America take a hard look at governmental operations as well as the political environment that affects them. A failure on the part of citizens to evaluate or analyze this environment is to accept the status quo without question. This lack of scrutiny sanctions a free pass to elected officials and government bureaucrats to continue the wasteful, impractical practices they seem so comfortable perpetuating.

If you believe there are things in government that need fixing, apathy cannot and will not help fix anything. Apathy will only prolong and even allow for the expansion of the corruption that should be obvious to those who possess a functioning mind. This apathy on the part of so many has resulted in the current governmental/political mess this nation faces.

Richard L. Freitag

Good Stuff

Whether happy or not with the present state of our government and the politics in this country, all citizens of these United States of America need to recognize that our constitutional republic form of government, implemented with democratic principles, is the best and most successful, time-tested form of government in the world today.

However, contrary to popular belief, our system of government is ***not a true democracy.*** If our system of government was indeed a true democracy, we would be subject to the will of the majority. This is the basis of a true democracy. We are ***not*** ruled by a majority.

We must understand that although there is certainly citizen participation in our form of government (making our government a ***form of*** democracy), we are not a pure democracy. Rather, we citizens of the United States of America are governed by a form of government known as a ***constitutional republic, which is defined as a government of LAW.*** In theory, in a constitutional republic, a single individual citizen can challenge our entire government using the courts of law. Therefore, a lone individual still counts. Every single citizen still remains a force to be dealt with in this country.

Over the past 225 years, this constitutional republic

has watched countless other forms of government fail around the world. While others have failed, we have not only survived and grown in significance and acceptance, but our form of government has become the envy of the rest of the world. Why is this?

This constitutional republic recognizes and upholds the ***individual citizen*** as the most significant factor in the entire governmental process. Though this concept of individuality has been under assault for the past several decades, this idea of individualism will not go away. The ideals of individual freedom, liberty, private property, and the possibility — but never a guarantee — for a lifetime of success and fulfillment by our own individual efforts are what make this nation unique. Combined with the free enterprise system, this form of government has resulted in the most good for the most people from its onset. No other nation on earth offers the opportunities to its citizens that this one does. **NOT ONE!** While not perfect, it is the best working model of a successful form of government in the world today.

So, if this constitutional republic is such a fine form of government with individual citizen involvement (democracy) that makes it truly a "government of the people, by the people, and for the people," what's to complain about? Why would anyone find fault with such a wonderful system of government? This is a fair question.

However, what if those who complain about government are not finding fault with the system of government? Instead, what if those who are not satisfied with the current situation in this nation's government were **not finding fault with the system of government** so much as they were at odds with ongoing corrupted **government systems?**

Or, what if those who are not happy with our present mess believe there is an undeniable, systematized failure on the part of the two major political parties to work in the best interests of the people they are elected to serve? What if the predominant complaint by those who are not satisfied with the status quo is that systematized politics needs both revision and improvement? What if the viewpoint is that without major change, there can only be disaster?

The Not So Good Stuff

"If it ain't broke, don't fix it."

This is the favorite argument of the less than concerned, or worse, the apathetic, mindless masses. At this point, the delusional are correct. It's true. It ain't broke — that is, **not totally broke.**

But do we need to wait until there is total collapse before corrective action is taken? How much longer can the belief that there is nothing wrong in government be tolerated by those of us who can see clearly? Should we simply accept the current level of wastefulness and corruption as do those who enable this madness to go on without voicing dissent? For those of us who do have the maturity to know that *problems do not simply go away, are we to remain mute?*

Of course, the underlying problem in a discussion of this nature is that first one must believe there are problems that exist in order that a remedy can be implemented, let alone discussed.

The apathetic masses with little care or concern for the future of this nation will agree our government has its faults, but they always are the first to allege that things are not all *that* bad. In discussions of concern for our nation's future, those who seem content with or unconcerned about our present political situation will routinely ask where you would rather live or what other nation you would rather be a citizen of.

Indeed, there is merit to this argument. Merit, that is, if you are happy with the unending waste, corruption, and fraud.

Many indifferent citizens believe all is well with the status quo. I can find no feeling of comfort in this argument when I view my government as out of control. Apparently the mindless seem to believe an out-of-control governmental mess is completely acceptable.

Richard L. Freitag

Those of us who are *not* happy and believe improvement is necessary if our government is to continue, ***do not find fault with our system of government. Rather, we find fault with governmental systems.***

Governmental systems are those continuing practices by government agencies, departments, and programs that are based solely on past practices, whether right or wrong (i.e. "that's how we've always done things"). Government agencies, departments, and programs need to be held up to the light of analysis, review, and scrutiny by the concerned citizenry.

A great many of these past practices are in serious need of basic justification for their very continuance and funding. A rudimentary review would likely reveal that many of our governments programs need to be discontinued. Questions need to be asked about why the existence of so many wasteful programs is tolerated.

All government programs are in need of cost analysis, and many need to be investigated for duplication and departmental overlap. Others need to have their purpose, if any can be found, questioned. What good is being done for the people for whom each program was initiated? How are the funds spent? What are the results of this spending?

All governmental entities need to be held accountable. Managers of government programs should be

The Citizens Initiative Party

forced to explain why certain ongoing practices are needed. Too many of these entrenched and legislatively protected government systems are perpetuated by career politicians and their bureaucratic lackeys for the sole purpose of political favor and re-election to office.

Without analysis and a thorough review of government programs, we continue to give a blank check to politicians and their bureaucratic minions who do *not* have a good track record when it comes to fiscal responsibility.

Our system of government is excellent; our governmental systems are foul!

IV. Triangulation

Navigators of old used an instrument called a sextant to find their way at sea. The instrument relied on triangulation to determine the ship's location.

Triangulation is a way of determining an unknown's location or course using the known locations of other things. Using two fixed or known positions, for instance a star and a land mass or two stars, mariners were able to fix their ship's location and determine its course.

Boy Scouts use triangulation to determine the height of objects, to estimate distance, or to fix a "point of origin" on a map for mapping and compass exercises. Triangulation can be described as a method of finding one's way.

But triangle — the root word of triangulation or triangulate — is always about three separate sides and three distinct points. Our founding fathers saw to it that three distinct branches of government were established, as stated in our national constitution. They created this three-part government structure to ensure a balance of power. In so doing, their thought was that no one branch of government would be able to become overly powerful and subdue the other two. There would be a system of checks and balances to prevent a power grab by any one branch of government.

The founders also decided there should be an odd number of justices on the Supreme Court, so as to prevent the possibility of deadlock and stalemate in our highest court.

These ideas were not arrived at by happenstance. Rather, sound, deliberate thinking with a clear vision of the future was used to make such determinations.

Let's see: a balance of power, a system of checks and balances to prevent a power grab, an odd number of branches of government, an odd number of justices. There is triangulation — a three-way split —in our government.

There is another consideration concerning the three-sided triangle. The triangle acts as a fulcrum — **the balance point**, for instance, of a scale.

Could this manner of thinking, this three-way approach to the political side of government, be made to work? Could three choices, rather than just two, have a positive effect on the political arena and create a positive change in the existing two political party system? Could three sides, three points of view be of benefit in the political environment? Could a permanent, major, third political party effect positive political change in the government?

Yes, it could!

Really?

Currently there are nearly fifty non-Democrat and non-Republican political parties already in operation. A fair question would be, why not simply make a few changes within one of these existing political organizations so that the political landscape of America could be altered for the better?

The answer is clear if you take a peripheral look at these existing third-party platforms and political positions. Basically, all of these third parties are radical in nature and have little to offer mainstream American citizens. For instance, there are the radical Socialists, radical environmentalists, gun control folks, agriculture advocates, radical labor people, radical this and radical that, but certainly all radical. There are neo-Nazis, Communists, pro-life and pro-abortion supporters, and really, there is even the Pot Party. There is something for everyone, from those advocating armed insurrection to those who seek a legalized "high."

Although you can choose to become a member of any of these parties, and certainly they'd all welcome your membership, be advised that none of these

The Citizens Initiative Party

micro-parties has ever made much of a difference in any election of the recent past, if at all.

Yet, there are two currently operating third parties that actually do make a showing and have a real influence on the political landscape. The first of these has been around a long time — **the Libertarian Party.** The other is a rather recent development on the political scene — **the Tea Party.**

The Libertarians have given a conservative voice to political issues for some time with little result, though they have actually run candidates under their banner.

The Tea Party is more of a conservative coalition or organization than an actual political party. This point is being made because the Tea Party has backed, endorsed, and supported candidates, but never actually run candidates under its banner.

While the Libertarians have made little political impact, the Tea Party people have actually made a significant impact on elections in the recent past.

But the point of all of this is: We need a new third party of broad appeal to all American citizens, especially those of the middle class, who are at present *not* politically represented. To build such a political party, we need to begin with a new, clean, fresh approach to politics and government.

V. Looking Back

A quick historical review of third-party activities during the 20th Century makes for a rather interesting study. Only once in a presidential election did just less than one in three voters vote for the third-party candidate. Once, just less than one in five voted for the third-party candidate. Twice, right around one in eight voted for the third-party candidate. Other than these four instances, third-party voting did not make even the slightest difference in the twenty-five national elections held during the 20th Century.

But why?

During the early years of the 20th Century, political unrest was due primarily to agricultural price declines, which gave rise to third-party organization and voting. There were all varieties of disgruntled farmers starting third parties for the express purpose of voicing opposition to a host of various perceived governmental and political injustices concerning farm commodity pricing. Most of these parties never had a national impact.

The Citizens Initiative Party

The best these political parties experienced were limited results in local, regional, or statewide campaigns.

The most successful third-party run for the presidency came in the 1912 election. Theodore Roosevelt ran on the Progressive Party (Bull Moose) ticket. Roosevelt's run for the presidency on a third-party ticket was nothing other than a personal vendetta waged by Roosevelt against then President William Howard Taft. Even though Taft was President Roosevelt's hand-picked successor at the end of Roosevelt's term as president, Taft did not carry out the programs as Roosevelt had wanted and envisioned. As a result, Roosevelt attacked his onetime friend with his 1912 third-party run for the presidency as an act of vengeance. This third-party attempt resulted in the election of Woodrow Wilson. The 1912 election results for Roosevelt hold the record for the greatest percentage of the popular vote ever cast for a third-party candidate — an amazing 27.39 percent.

The second-best showing for a third-party candidate belongs to businessman H. Ross Perot in his 1992 presidential run. Perot and his Reform Party captured just over 19 percent of the popular vote.

Unfortunately, H. Ross Perot *was* the party, and his run for the presidency was the sole reason for the existence of the Reform Party. Mr. Perot ran for the presidency again in 1996, but didn't have as good a result as he had in the previous election. With the end of the 1996 campaign, Mr. Perot was no longer involved with the party he had originated, and like most other third parties of the 20th Century, the Reform Party simply faded away.

Third place for third parties in politics belongs to Robert La Follette. His Progressive Party run for the presidency in the election of 1924 captured 16.56 percent of the popular vote.

Fourth place in third-party voting records belongs to George Wallace and his American Independent Party in his 1968 bid for the presidency. Unbelievably, the segregationist Wallace received 13.53 percent of the popular vote for his efforts.

Other than John Anderson, an independent, who captured 6.61 percent of the popular vote in the 1980 presidential election, all other attempts by third parties for our nation's top elected office have resulted in, at best, around 3 percent or less of the popular vote.

All of these third-party attempts have involved a run for the presidency of the United States and little else. There has never really been a sustained effort by any third party to elect candidates to the House of Representatives or the Senate, let alone state and local runs.

In recent years, there has been one independent U.S. senator, Joe Lieberman of Connecticut, a former

The Citizens Initiative Party

Democrat who remains closely tied to the Democratic Party, and perhaps one or so independent congressmen and a state governor or two. There are no other non-Democrats or non-Republicans holding national or state elected office.

There remains one very interesting political phenomenon concerning third-party voting and third-party candidates for office during the 20th Century. Minnesota actually elected a third-party candidate to the office of governor in 1998. Jesse Ventura, a former professional wrestler and mayor of the Twin Cities suburb of Brooklyn Park, Minnesota, rejuvenated the Reform Party and captured the state's top elected office.

Governor Ventura, while an interesting political anomaly, is indicative of what can and will happen to third-party candidates who are successful in gaining top, executive-level offices. Without the support of other members of their political party — people who share their political viewpoint and philosophy — third-party candidates elected to leadership positions are doomed to ineffectiveness from the beginning of their elected term. As was the case for Governor Ventura, a few pieces of legislation brought forth by the elected leader were passed initially during the "honeymoon period" of his term. But after those first few legislative successes, members of both of the major parties did everything in their power to make certain that Governor Ventura was a one-termer. Ventura was constantly reminded that he was not a member in good standing of either the Democratic or Republican Party. He was completely stifled in his attempts to lead.

Though a non-Democrat or non-Republican may have good intentions and visionary ideas and be duly elected by the populace, as was Governor Ventura, without the support of like-minded party members in the legislative branch of any government body — state or national — the third-party political leader will be rendered completely ineffective by both Democrats and Republicans.

In a rare instance of bipartisan cooperation, members of both of the major parties will work together to make certain that this third-party official and his party are made to look the fool. The intention of this bipartisan effort is that there will be no further growth in numbers of these third-party radicals and their ideas.

The lesson here is that third-party candidates need friendly faces in the legislative branch to support the ideas of the elected leader in our democratic, elected form of government.

Only dictatorships run by edict need no friendly faces. They need only fear of reprisal for those who don't support the leader's ideas. We don't need a dictatorship.

The Citizens Initiative Party

Back to Governor Ventura ….

Ventura's election campaign was a treat to watch. Living near the Minnesota/Wisconsin border, I found it was fun to observe this three-way campaign first hand. Candidate Ventura offered some interesting ideas concerning taxation, as well as other novel ideas. It was exciting to watch Jesse Ventura in action during the several televised governor candidate debate forums. Ventura basically sat there listening to both of his political rivals pound on one another. He said very little while his opponents tore each other apart. Both of the candidates Ventura faced had their own problems, and he was wise enough to not say much at all. He shrewdly let the two major party candidates destroy one another. It was a thing of beauty indeed.

As mentioned, both of the major party candidates had their own problems. One of the players had all the charm, personality, and charisma of a brick. The other candidate, who quit the Democratic party so he could take a run at the office of governor, left the voting public wondering where he stood politically and just what, other than a political animal, he was all about.

Jesse Ventura's basic appeal to the voting public was this: "Look, if you don't want either of these babbling idiots to head up your state's government, I'll be honored to serve as Minnesota's top elected official." This simple strategy worked. Ventura was elected governor.

After his election, Governor Ventura was allowed by the legislature to restructure Minnesota's rather high-priced motor vehicle license plate fee schedule structure. The revised fee schedule approached normalcy (even for Minnesota) under Ventura's leadership.

The governor's next move was to establish an urban mass transit system for the metropolitan Twin Cities called the Light Rail Transit System. This mass transit system had been talked about for years, but never acted upon in the legislature. Both Republicans and Democrats feared introducing the legislation to create such a system, just in case this new mass transit system didn't work out well. Such a proposal could become a political pariah for the political party or politician who introduced the idea. As a result, not one member of either of the major parties had the guts to initiate or to back anyone forming a coalition to make the system possible. Prior to Ventura, the fear of failure dictated that the legislation never happened, and, therefore, no mass transit legislation was ever introduced.

Once Governor Jesse Ventura demonstrated the guts, drive, vision, and initiative to introduce legislation to make possible the Light Rail Transit System, (remember, this was during the "honeymoon" period) both Democrats and Republicans, in a rare bipartisan effort, backed

The Citizens Initiative Party

the legislation and passed it. Of course, the real reason for this bipartisan effort on the part of the membership of the Republicans and the Democrats was the hope that passage of this legislation would politically take down Governor Ventura. But the elected membership of both the Republican Party and their Democratic Party co-conspirators got it wrong.

As it turns out, the Light Rail Transit System is a tremendous success story in the Minneapolis and St. Paul, Minnesota, metropolitan area. This mass transit system is in fact such a success story that the system has been expanded a couple of times. Currently, several suburban metro area communities are linked into the system, with plans for others joining in the future. Nothing would have come of this marvelous mass transit system success story had it not been for Governor Ventura's leadership and courage. The Twin Cities' Light Rail Transit System stands as this nation's lone tribute to a third-party politician with the vision, integrity, and character to make a positive difference for the populace he was elected to serve.

Sadly, after the passage of the Light Rail Transit System legislation, Governor Ventura was able to effect few other positive changes for Minnesota. Even with appeals for support from the voting public, many of his proposed visionary changes died for lack of support. Fearing the governor might experience too much success or gain in popularity, the equally cowardly Democrats and Republicans joined forces to place roadblocks in the path of any further legislative initiatives by Ventura. They would show this third-party upstart his proper place. As a result, any other legislative innovation and creativity that might have taken place under the governor's leadership was terminated. Gutless Democrats and Republicans, fearing that other of the governor's ideas might well have merit in the public eye, shut Ventura down. After all, if he were too successful, they would be exposed for their lack of leadership, their failure as visionaries, and their ineptitude in general. All of this would leave the major party candidates vulnerable in the next election. Here then is a rare situation in which members of both of the major political parties joined forces to work together for the sole purpose of rendering a real leader from a third party powerless.

How much do you love politics and politicians when it appears that the purpose of holding an elected office is not to serve the public, but rather to merely get re-elected or destroy creativity?

The real problem confronting elected Republicans and Democrats was that, even though they didn't know how successful the governor might be, they couldn't afford to take the risk that his ideas would be or could be worthwhile. Or worse yet, he could make a positive difference in the lives of the citizens of Minnesota. It was nothing other than fear — the fear of success for a third-party operative — that cut the governor out of the legislative process altogether. Could elected Democrats and Republicans perhaps have been afraid that another legislative success by Governor Ventura would cause voting citizens to take another look at the viability of other third-party candidates?

Tragically, Governor Jesse Ventura of Minnesota became the target of a media feeding frenzy. Once cut out of the legislative process by career Democratic and Republican politicians, his time of making a positive difference and serving the people of Minnesota came to an end. Once removed from the legislative process by the legislature that feared him, he started to referee wrestling matches and became a commentator for football games. The media, possibly, worked along with their Democratic and Republican friends at making the governor look like a buffoon. Critics had a heyday.

After being reduced to a non-element in the political process, why would Ventura not choose to do other things with his time? His power and political position, which could have effected other positive changes for his state and its citizens, had been thwarted by those who were seeking nothing other than to maintain, preserve, and protect the status quo they so enjoyed.

And yet, Governor Ventura's legacy will not go away. He stands alone as the one bright, shining star that broke the barrier of the two-party system. For those of us who hold that a new direction for government can be brought about only by the formation of a new third party, Minnesota's Governor Jesse Ventura is a true hero and a much needed breath of fresh air.

Many thanks to you for your fine example and inspired leadership when allowed, Governor Ventura!

Looking back on the 20th Century, of all third-party candidates, really only one could have pushed through any of his programs and legislative initiatives on the national level — Theodore Roosevelt. At the time he ran as the presidential candidate of a third party, he was well-known to the general population and the elected officials serving the Senate and the House of Representatives because he had been president prior to Taft. Using a combination of the force of his will, his dynamic personality, and his immense popularity, the 26th president alone could have effected positive change by popular appeal. Had Theodore Roosevelt become the first-ever elected third-party president, this monumental occasion may well have given rise to a prolonged third-party presence.

Governor Ventura's record of legislative stalemate

The Citizens Initiative Party

for most of his term in office serves as the only example we have to demonstrate what happens when non-Republican or non-Democratic leaders are elected. No elected official should need to suffer through a term in office without being able to effect at least some change. Without the support of a functioning political party and without any friends in the legislature, little will be allowed to happen by the two major parties. Ventura had noble intentions and some very innovative and novel ideas. Yet, one individual with nonexistent support and without any political party backing whatsoever can do little to affect the much-needed changes in governmental systems.

Can you imagine how effective four years of the leadership of President H. Ross Perot might have been when there were 535 members of either the Republican or Democratic Parties and no Reform Party members serving in the legislative branch of the government? Members of both major political parties would have devoted **all** of their time and **all** of their energy to making certain that President Perot was "put in his place" and hog-tied legislatively.

They would have made him understand he was unwelcome as a leader because he was a member of a third political party and not a member of either of theirs. For Democrats and Republicans alike, the combined policy would have been that the people and their interests be damned. They would have devoted themselves to making sure this "upstart" was unable to enjoy success at any cost.

To summarize the results of third-party efforts during the 20th Century, it is very evident even in the most successful case — the election of Governor Ventura — that any elected third-party official will need the full weight of a party organization backing that elected leader. In addition, that third-party elected leader will need the company and support of other members of the party in the legislative branch of the government who share a similar philosophy and vision for the future.

The lesson here for those of us interested in making a third party become reality is that we will need to focus our beginning efforts at local and state levels. We will need to elect party members to boards and councils or, at the state and national levels, to legislative offices. Until we are a well-established political force, we need to recognize that going for top executive positions in state or national elections will only render our elected party member powerless in the face of overwhelming numbers of existing major party members in the legislative branch.

VI. Looking Ahead

We are told America's population is aging. Demographic studies of our nation made by bona fide researchers confirm that this is true.

While it may be true that we as a nation are growing older, it seems we are ***politically reluctant*** to:
- ▶ act in a mature, adult-like manner.
- ▶ deal comfortably within the realm of facts.
- ▶ face reality.
- ▶ quit making excuses.
- ▶ quit blaming others.
- ▶ be responsible for our own life.
- ▶ embrace independence.
- ▶ cherish our freedom.

It's time to WAKE UP!
It's time to GROW UP!

Until and unless we, as concerned citizens of this nation, ***grow up*** politically so that we can come to grips with the reality and the magnitude of the political and fiscal problems we face, we need to be prepared to hang on for a terrible time ahead. Without a mature, grown-up approach to solve the problems this nation faces, get ready for a massive fiscal calamity of disastrous proportions. And, given the current political climate, it will get worse as time progresses.

You think some of the European Union countries have problems? What do you think things might look like when the world's largest economy goes down? What happens to the United States of America when the total tax revenues will be used up completely to pay for nothing other than the interest on our ballooning national debt?

Is it a politically responsible act for the membership of the two major parties to continue to allow for an increase in the national debt while doing nothing to curb spending? And both parties are equally responsible for this looming disaster. Is a philosophy and belief in the possibility of **borrowing our way out of debt** truly sound judgment made by truly mature elected officials? How long must we endure this madness before our house-of-cards fiscal policy comes crashing down?

In the absence of a new, major third political party, the political gridlock and stalemate that has taken this nation to the precipice of fiscal disaster can only and will only be allowed to continue. Of course, there are those who delight in the prospect of such a scenario. They are card-carrying members of the Democratic and Republican parties.

There are those who claim that political stalemate is just fine. The belief is that under stalemated conditions, elected officials can't do as much damage politically. They may well have a good point. But realistically, what a sad situation indeed! It's MBE (male bovine excrement)!

What about those of us who are not happy with this political impasse? It's probably not the best-case scenario when political gridlock becomes the accepted goal. Wouldn't you like to believe that elected government officials are voted into office so they can legislate on the people's behalf?

Enacting legislation takes action. Action does not happen, by definition, in an environment of gridlock or stalemate.

So … what to do? Are we, as a nation, indeed at a time and place in our history with a real need to try to "find our way" politically? And is it true that we presently have two very inflexible points of view concerning our nation's future? And if those fixed points are known (I think both parties have expressed their positions in very strong terms), I'd like to suggest *triangulation* as our best bet for finding our way amid this clouded political/governmental mess.

We need a third party!

Richard L. Freitag

Actions taken by a third party, if properly orchestrated, will end the stalemate. A third party will need to be dealt with by the two major parties, and this will force political movement that will end the gridlock. To move any legislation through the legislative branch of government, political coalitions would need to be formed once there are three parties, not just two.

Three-way representation of the electorate on the floor of the House of Representatives and the Senate certainly will change political dynamics. Once the real presence of a third party that the major party elected leadership would be forced to deal with was established, some very interesting political maneuvering would have to transpire.

At present, we have only one example of such a situation. Minnesota Senator Paul Wellstone (D-MN) perished in an airplane crash when Jesse Ventura was the governor of Minnesota. With Senator Wellstone's passing, Governor Ventura was tasked with appointing a replacement for Wellstone until the end of Wellstone's elected term in office. Governor Ventura appointed Dean Barkley, who was a non-Democrat/non-Republican. The pandering to Barkley by Senate members of both major political parties was most interesting to observe. Democrats and Republicans didn't know what to do with this guy. They were at a loss, because they

The Citizens Initiative Party

wanted his support but couldn't figure out how to work with a senator who was a member of neither of their parties. Leadership of both parties was in the habit of using bullying tactics to force freshman senators to see things their way. Barkley couldn't be bullied because he wasn't a member of either party.

Because of this situation, Democrats and Republicans were forced to deal with Senator Dean Barkley in a manner they weren't used to. And, it was impossible for members of the major parties to simply dismiss this non-major party member of the Senate. Rather than simply ignoring or brushing Barkley aside, it was necessary to "court" him in the interest of gaining his support. So the major party players tripped over themselves to gain Barkley's backing.

Just think how wonderful it would be to have a number of Barkley-like elected officials in the Senate and the House of Representatives. No longer would the political wrangling be a tug-of-war between two opponents. (Actually, the present situation is about as effective as ***pushing on a rope*** as opposed to pulling.) Rather, two-against-one political coalitions would need to be formed to enact any legislation at all.

If and when this three-party political configuration is developed, true political posturing and genuine negotiation would take place by necessity. The result would be real political action. This would break the stalemate.

This newfound formation of coalitions would necessitate political action, political negotiation, and political compromise. Such coalition-forming political activity would certainly jump-start the end of the present political gridlock.

VII. Stagecoach

Without a doubt, one of America's great movie actor icons is the late, great John Wayne. Wayne's first ever starring role was in the circa 1939 American Western film classic *Stagecoach,* directed by legendry film director John Ford. John Wayne's portrayal of the Ringo Kid in *Stagecoach* launched a starring role cinema career of unprecedented magnitude and longevity. With many scenes of the movie filmed in the majestic Monument Valley, *Stagecoach* stood as the bar by which future Westerns would be judged.

The story line of the film revolves around a group of nine strangers thrown together in a stagecoach traveling in the old Southwest from Tonto, Arizona, to Lordsburg, New Mexico. As in every good American film with a Western theme, there is group interaction between the good guys and the bad guys. All sorts of adventures of either a dangerous or comical nature take place during the movie. It is action-packed and is true Americana at its best.

During the trip there are a few stagecoach stops. Here the passengers disembark for a stretch or sit down for a meal at a table laden with food lovingly prepared by the kind-hearted wife of the station manager. Various conversational interactions take place among the guests at the table.

Although a stretch, a hearty meal, or other necessities may well be among the reasons for the stagecoach to stop, there is another big reason. While the guests are at the table feasting, the stagecoach station manager and the driver are out in the yard at work watering and feeding the horses to keep them healthy. And at certain stations, **changing the team** of horses is imperative so the stagecoach can continue on with a totally fresh team.

A ***fresh team*** of horses is necessary to keep up the pace of the stagecoach, which must run with integrity on a specific time schedule from city to city.

Changing the Team

No team of horses can pull a stagecoach forever. Even though watered and fed, there comes a time when the team of horses needs to be changed. After a while, the team is tired, exhausted, and worn out. The horses have done their duty. They are removed from their task.

If stagecoach drivers and station managers back in the Old West were smart enough to know there existed a need for a change every so often even for lowly draft animals after a certain length of service, why are we, the voting public, so foolish as to allow tired, exhausted, worn-out legislators to serve indefinitely? How effective can an antique legislator be when allegedly serving his constituents while in a comatose state? (YES! This has been the case.)

Was political service and politics intended to be a career by the founders of our nation? No, it certainly wasn't. Elected public office was intended to be a temporary calling — an opportunity to serve, but never a lifetime's work.

Since there is a term limit for the chief executive of this nation, certainly there should be term limits on all other elected offices, including judgeships, as well. Term limits should be imposed at all levels of government — national, state, and local. If elected officials are so incompetent that they are unable to accomplish their political goals as a U.S. senator in two six-year terms or as a member of the House of Representatives in six two-year terms, they should be sent home "for cause" in any event.

After completing two six-year Senate terms, a former senator who felt a need for continued public service could change tracks and run as a congressman, or vice versa. Or these "termed out" officials could choose to go back to their state and run for state office positions. Or, they could do something worthwhile such as take a real job or go into business.

If "termed out" on the state level, and if the official didn't want to move up to the national level, the politician could go home and run for dog catcher if he or she found elected office to be mandatory for self-fulfillment.

But after twelve years, just like tired, exhausted, worn-out horses, elected officials need to be "put in the barn" or "put out to pasture" — but at the very least **PUT OUT!**

After twelve years of service, the likelihood of elected officials having any reserve muscle for the work at hand, let alone visionary ideas or novel thoughts, is remote at best. While there may be certain antique legislators with sharp minds, they are few indeed.

To the horses' credit, after being in the harness for an extended period of time, they didn't become aloof and arrogant. Far too many elected officials seem to take on these traits over time when they have held office for too long. While the horses continue to understand their duty and perform that duty, so many politicians forget who is supposed to be working for whom.

Too many of these arrogant, conceited, narcissistic politicians view themselves as above reproach and above the law, or so it would appear. Haughtiness, self-righteousness, and an outright disdain for those who elected them to serve in the first place are all too common among long-serving politicians. What should be viewed as a temporary opportunity to serve the electorate becomes a lifelong, self-justified career. This situation may no longer be of benefit to the electorate, but it remains a benefit to the politician and the politician's wallet.

Narcissism lends itself well to justification of political corruption, self-indulgence, and supposed self-righteous validation for that which otherwise would be considered "bad form." A review of past practices and recent history has shown that when one becomes so self-important and so self-righteous, it is a rather simple matter to justify whatever form of foul activity the self-serving politician can deem to be acceptable behavior.

As an example, recently we've had a congressman wake up one morning to discover that he owned a half-million dollar home in the Dominican Republic! Until that morning, supposedly, he had no idea of the existence of this place. Since he had no idea that he owned the place which he didn't know existed, he had neglected to pay taxes on the income he used to make the purchase he didn't know he had made. Go figure. But, it's all okay since he didn't know. MBE!

Other elected officials find it's okay to have the

taxpayer pick up the tab for their personal air travel back and forth to their homes in Western states. How very cheap of these conceited, arrogant, self-righteous, self-appointed, super-important, so-called "public servants." When hearing of the costs involved in these taxpayer-funded fiascoes, a fair question again becomes, who is serving whom in these cases?

Concerning elected officials and their perks, especially at the national level, should politicians really be entitled to a lavish retirement program and a health care program that we mere citizens could not even dream of? Unless these elected officials are exceedingly special, exceptionally great and mighty, or extremely all-important, why should they not have the same health care that they insist is just great for all the rest of the population?

But wait. There's more. These elected officials — the self-important and self-righteous — are rewarded for their seniority with re-election and the "chair" positions on prestigious and powerful committees in the House of Representatives and the Senate, based on seniority alone. At present, given the accepted "business as usual" mentality, the longer these relics hang around in office, regardless of their diminished mental capacity, limited ingenuity, innovation or creativity, the more powerful they become politically. As a result of their political power based entirely on seniority, the electorate back at home cannot afford to give up this political power and influence granted to senior members of both houses of Congress. Senior members have power. The newly elected members have none. Because of this seniority system, crooks and scoundrels are re-elected time after time to protect the power and influence of the states or congressional districts from which they are elected.

Currently, committee "chairs" are held only by the most senior member of any given committee. But if the governmental system of tenure or seniority were ended, how could the various committees within Congress possibly determine who should hold the "chair" of all of the various committees? How could this systematized mess be altered for the betterment of the nation?

The answer is simple if the concept of term limits becomes the law of the land. When term limits for **all** elected officials are made the law of the land, after the formation of the various committees, the membership of each of these committees would hold an election for the "chair" position. The "chair" position would then go to that member who had the most experience, knowledge, background, education, and expertise in the given field of endeavor of that committee. For instance, a medical doctor might head up the Health, Education, and Welfare Committee. A former trucking company executive might head up the Transportation Committee, etc.

Wouldn't that be a change? Just think of it. A committee chairperson would have real knowledge and background and expertise in his or her area of governance! Could such a system possibly work? Could the government be improved by having elected officials with real knowledge and experience in the area of their committees' responsibilities actually heading up operations? Or do we simply continue on with the **antiquated political hacks** we presently have, who continue to make feeble attempts at trying to act knowledgeable while continuing to legislate some of the dumbest stuff imaginable?

What is your feeling in this regard?

Let's work to end the narcissism, arrogance, and self-righteousness of elected officials. Let's work together to stop the corruption and terminate the stupidity. There is a better way.

Term limits on elected officials would make a positive change!

VIII. Beautiful Garden

A number of my friends, like many Americans, enjoy gardening. They take pride in the produce and/or flowers they grow in their gardens. So many of these gardens are works of art to be viewed and enjoyed not only by the gardener, but by passers-by and neighbors alike.

Every spring, gardeners purchase seeds or plants, work the soil, and labor long and hard to make the gardening process work. After the plants have sprouted, the gardeners continue to weed and water the plants to ensure they stay healthy. The red tomatoes, the bright greens, yellows and oranges of various peppers, the healthy potatoes, carrots, lettuce, turnips, and of course, the spectacular colors of the many different flowers are a sight to behold and the source of pride the gardener envisioned back at planting time.

So many of the gardeners I know enjoy sharing, literally, "the fruits of their labors" with friends, relatives and neighbors. Not only do they share their produce and flowers, they share with the recipients of these gifts their sense of accomplishment. Their pride in their work is reflected in the high quality and near perfection of these gifts of food and beauty they willingly share with others. Gardens, gardeners, and gardening are beautiful things.

But, what if after the gardener makes the investment in the seed, does all of the labor and, through these efforts, has success in growing plants to be proud of, this garden is invaded by a band of marauding wild hogs? The hogs rip the place apart and devour the produce. They smash or eat the flowers and turn what had been a thing of beauty into an area of devastation and ugliness.

The gardener is no longer able to share the produce and flowers with friends and neighbors. Unfortunately, the hard-working gardener's only hope is that the greedy hogs have left enough of the products of his labor to feed his immediate family. Sharing is no longer an option. The wild hogs with their voracious, insatiable appetites have ruined any thought of sharing or giving.

The investment and labor are an ***individual effort,*** and the risk and potential reward are personal sacrifices of ***individual choice,*** so the rewards of these efforts and the related choice of how to share these rewards ***should go to that individual who made the effort, did the work, and took the risk.***

Once the wild hogs have devoured the produce, there is no getting that produce back. Had the hogs contributed to the effort of growing the garden, it would be different. But the wild hogs only take. They contribute nothing. The wild hogs remove any thought of sharing with others, because the produce is gone, and the only certainty about it is that the devoured produce will be turned into pig poop.

Of course, there are those who will argue the value of pig poop. These are the same folks who can't or won't come to grips with the big picture. What had once been a source of pride and workmanship and could have been shared with others has been turned into pig poop. There was a time when I personally would have been happy to share the pig poop with those who can't see the reality of the devastation wrought by the marauding wild hogs. But not anymore.

When deprived of our option to share whatever we choose with whomever we choose, we have lost that which is, and should be, our choice alone. When an individual makes the decision of what and with whom to share the fruits of their labor, this is what defines our personal generosity and our ability to be philanthropic. When deprived of our ability to make choices, even though we may wish to be generous, we simply can't do it. There's nothing left for us to give, because what we had wished to give or share has been taken from us by others. The garden is ruined. The ability and choice to be generous has been taken from us. As a result, *no one can give away, share, or invest what has been confiscated from them.*

By definition, generosity is not and cannot be forced upon any individual. Forced sharing is **confiscation and redistribution. *This is communism!*** Individuals no longer have any choice. Neither do they have the funding to back their choice with regard to generosity and sharing. This is MBE (male bovine excrement)!

The marauding band of wild hogs destroying the garden is not at all unlike the government when, through excessive taxation and redistribution of wealth, it deprives individuals of what they have earned by their individual efforts. Those who argue that raising taxes (taking away what the individual has earned by their efforts and investment alone) is a good thing are the same people who would argue about all the good there is in pig poop. When the income individuals have earned is taken from them, it is turned into its own form of pig poop — ***government waste.***

Have you ever challenged the well-intentioned, yet obviously naive dreamers to share their knowledge about any and all government programs they believe are well-run, practical, and efficient operations? Let them respond with facts about all such programs — all of them. Yes, that's right, as usual you too will get the "deer eyes in the headlights" response. Yet these are the same folks who refuse to deal with reality and persist in calling for more and more meaningless government programs funded by higher and higher taxes. The best response to the obviously naive is "***Grow up! Face reality! Quit with the MBE already!***" The most dangerous element in these dreamers' political position arises when they can no longer differentiate between dreams and reality. Far too many on the far left suffer from this sickness.

But then, to the purest of the dreamers, taxation always is about taking from somebody else — ***but not them!*** Given this attitude toward taxation, why wouldn't ***everybody*** be in favor of raising taxes? Oops, that's right. Within the group titled ***"everybody,"*** there are those somebodies who actually have to pay the taxes because, in the real world, somebody has to pay. Therefore, within the "everybody who is in favor of raising taxes" group, there is a subgroup of the **"somebodies" who will need to pay the taxes!**

So many non-realists enjoy speaking about equality, justice and fairness — all noble concepts, certainly. What about practicing what they are preaching? Wouldn't it be wonderful if the dreamers demonstrated some consistency? That is to say, if dreamers think paying taxes is such a great idea, go ahead — pay all you want. Show the rest of us who don't think paying taxes is such a wonderful idea where your heart is. Lead by example. Send *extra* funds to the IRS. You know it will be spent wisely. Fortunately for the dreamers and the others on the far left, I have an idea for consideration.

But first a couple of questions concerning taxation; Are our current tax laws fair to all? And, could our tax laws be made any more intricate, confusing, and complex?

If equality, justice, and fairness are noble concepts, it seems to me that the only truly fair taxation policy has *all* members of society contributing by equal measure. That is to say, all will pay an *equal percentage of earnings.* Just so the do-gooders can feel good about this taxation idea, we'll call it the **Equal Tax** or **= Tax. Now,** *all will pay equally* **and no one — *no one* — will be either exempt from taxation nor will anyone be afforded special treatment because of their social, financial, or any other status within our society.** Any thresholds or baselines will be applied to all taxpayers. In other words, if do-gooders wish to establish a threshold of, say $40,000, the first $40,000 of income will be tax exempt for all. There will be an end to this silly and most arbitrary discussion concerning "ability to pay." All taxpayers would pay equally. Not the same amount certainly, but the people living under the bridge (because that bridge is provided at taxpayer expense) will pay the same percentage as those living in the castle on the hill. So, if your ability to pay is low and you don't like it, it's up to *you* to change your income status to remedy your financial situation. In the real world, there is no one else, other than you, who can or will change your financial situation for you.

This is pure equality, pure justice and absolute fairness! And it's simple! The best part of all is that this system would completely remove *politics* from taxation policy.

But this idea is not something new. It is only a re-labeling in an attempt to be politically correct for the do-gooders. (After all, don't you just love do-gooders and "political correctness"?) This idea was proposed some time ago by Steve Forbes. Read *Flat Tax Revolution: Using a Postcard to Abolish the IRS* (Regnery Publishing Inc. 2005)

But what if taxation were simplified to this level? Everybody, without exception, would be responsible for and take ownership in the tax burden! What if all had to pay without regard to their income level? And, what if at the same time, all citizens could readily understand the tax laws without needing professional help? But then, what would become of all the tax preparers?

Richard L. Freitag

Here is an idea. While there will continue to be a need for accountants in the areas of business and finance, all non-business accountants, CPAs and tax preparation specialists could become independent contractors. Their talents could be employed to be watch dogs for government entities. They could bid on the audit work for all government agencies from the local sewage district up to and including the national Department of Defense. They would be paid a percentage of the waste, fraud, misappropriations and mismanagement of funds they discover or uncover. Certainly, they'd all be wealthy in no time!

Of course, the problem with accounting is that it happens "after the fact." The damage has already been done. The theft or waste is complete by the time the accountants look back in time to discover the misdeeds. As an example, look at what happens as a result of all the fiscal analysis done by the Government Accountability Office (GAO). By the time their reports of wrongdoing are presented, the wrongful act is history. The money has vanished and they have moved on to the next investigation, which will also produce piles of paperwork but no positive, concrete results. Aren't you delighted that we have the GAO?

But the problem is not just wasteful government programs. The real problem is that there is absolutely

The Citizens Initiative Party

no — ***none as in nonexistent*** — accountability nor oversight of government spending. And, as always, no one in government is ever responsible. No one in government is ever required to answer questions. Nobody in government ever has their "feet held to the fire" and certainly no one in government is ever fired, disciplined, or fined for their actions or inactions. Never!

Then too, there is this great oxymoron, "government management." I have personal experience in what "government management" means.

Just a quick but true personal story;

I was invited by the facility manager of a smaller-sized federal installation to bid on a landscape maintenance and repair project. I arrived and met with the manager, who informed me he wanted all of the turf in a certain area of the facility removed and replaced with new sod. I said I noticed on my way into the building how great his turf looked and that it was probably one of the finest-looking lawn areas I'd ever seen. He said, "Never mind that. I want it all removed, hauled away, and replaced with new turf grass." So I dutifully went out and measured the area to figure my project bid price.

When back in his office, I asked, "What's going on? What's wrong with the most perfect-looking turf I've seen in a long time?" He pointed out that the grass was not the problem. He informed me that the real issue was that he had a *surplus of funds* in his annual budget. If he underspent his annual budget, he would not be allotted the same level of funding in next year's budget. And certainly, should there be funds left over in his budget, there would be absolutely no possibility of a budgetary increase for the maintenance of this facility.

As a private industry businessman, I certainly wasn't comfortable with his reasoning and related that to him. His reply was, "Let me put it to you this way. I called you first because you have an excellent reputation. Also, the word on the street is that you are a little higher priced than your competitors. Now either you are going to do this work or your competitors are going to do the work, but *the work will be done* and *my remaining funds will go away.* Do you understand? Now are you interested in the project or not? If you are interested, what is your price?"

Baffled, I gave him a price which he, in turn, said needed to be increased in order to zero out his budget. I did do the work, justifying it by telling myself that it would provide work for my crew and deny my competitors the project and resulting income. Was it right? No, but that's business.

Obviously, no one can make up a crazy story like this. But just think of the big picture here. This incident happened at a rather small federal facility with one so-called manager. Think of the larger government facilities or the huge governmental departments. All of them, in terms of fiscal responsibility, are managed in the same manner.

As a former small businessman, it is difficult at best and more likely impossible to wrap my mind around calling this type of thinking "management" in any way, shape, or form. A five- or six-year-old child is capable of this kind of so-called "management." To the government, management means just "blow" all your funds. Or, better yet, if you're a really great manager, exceed your budget. A failure to do so on the part of the so-called manager will result in budgetary punishment for both department and department head in the next budgetary period. Apparently, if you are a truly stellar manager, you exceed your budget on a regular basis so that you can get an annual budget increase year after year. Imagine this mind-set.

This practice is a completely foreign and totally bizarre concept to those of us who are not government employees or government managers. While saving, frugality, and responsible spending are concepts **mandatory** for the rest of us, they appear to be unknown to government managers. Be it our business or our household, we would be broke and/or bankrupt and living under a bridge if we managed our money and our budgets in the manner in which our government manages theirs. And the real problem is that it's *our* money they are wasting!

But, what if government managers were rewarded for the surpluses left in their operating budgets? What if they were rewarded with a small portion of a percentage of the surplus funds left over as an acknowledgement of the good stewardship of funds entrusted to their care? The fractional percentage need not be all that much. Just think if there would be a surplus left over in the budgets of the Department of Defense, the Department of Energy, the Department of Homeland Security just to name a few. A mere sliver of a fraction of a single percent could amount to millions of dollars for said manager or department head. Perhaps as an option, these surplus funds could remain in a "rainy day" account within the well managed department.

If such a radical concept were introduced into the system of government management, I'll guarantee (and I know you can see it too), that suddenly, wasteful spending would be eliminated. There would be genuine incentives to cut costs and look at operations in an analytical manner for a change. Just imagine real cost analysis and real efficiency studies and real spending reductions made by real managers working for our government. Can you imagine?

Yet this radical concept begs the question. What about the unscrupulous public official who might

The Citizens Initiative Party

be financially induced to curtail spending simply to increase personal reward at the expense of public need? Or to put it another way, under a personal reward system for prudent management such as this one proposed, would management-level decisions be made entirely on the basis of personal reward? For example, is it possible that a dilapidated, dangerous old bridge needing replacement for safety reasons be postponed or delayed by a money-hungry public official seeking personal reward? This is a fair question.

First, let us understand and agree that there will always remain a stark distinction with regard to the difference between true need and necessity versus increased efficiency or waste elimination.

As such, any public official who would attempt to sidestep real needs and necessities would be subject to criminal prosecution in the name of negligence of the public safety.

Without a doubt though, in some cases, certainly there will be willful disregard for those whom these public officials are hired to serve. Such disregard for those whom they serve may well result in disgusting scenarios and things of this nature may well happen in certain instances. However, this sort of borderline criminal behavior on the part of public officials would be short-lived. Given a politically aroused citizenry per the definition of "citizen" by Pericles, the corrupt public official would not last long. There would be criminal charges leveled against such corrupt individuals. Their ability to blame others for their errors and their greed, to disavow their responsibility and so forth, would end their careers quickly. More on this in Chapter XIII.

Just one final prophetic analogy on this topic. It comes from my past when I was engaged in the business of transporting hay from Kansas and Nebraska to Wisconsin to keep area dairy herds in milk production. I was unloading a semi load of hay at my biggest customer's farm one day. He was one of the smartest men I ever met in my entire life.

Give what he said to me that day so long ago some serious thought. Just like the socioeconomic makeup of American Society news report mentioned earlier, I just can't get this out of my mind.

As we were unloading the load of hay, he said to me, "You know, I've been thinking about what's going on here, and it just doesn't make any sense at all. As a matter of fact, it's not wise."

I asked, "What do you mean, John?"

He replied, "Take a real look at what we are doing here from my point of view. I'm getting this hay from you to feed to these animals which in turn will grow bigger so that they eat up more hay. Now you show me or explain to me the wisdom in this."

In this story, substitute the word "taxes" for the word "hay" and substitute the word "government" for the word "animals." Then, think about what John said to me.

Think About It!

If government had a better track record of stewardship for funds it collects from the tax paying public, we the taxpayers would probably feel a whole lot better about paying taxes to the government. Given their disgusting track record, elected officials and bureaucrats within government will first need to demonstrate their sincerity with regard to good stewardship of funds entrusted to them by the public. They will need to make the first move in this regard.

Before there can ever be a positive change in the attitude of the taxpaying public, there will need to be a ***true demonstration of real spending reduction*** by the government. Not just talk and more MBE, but real spending reduction.

In the absence of true spending reduction, taxpayers who despise paying taxes will never find comfort in sending more and more money to government officials whom these taxpayers believe will waste these precious funds.

Those of us who do not and cannot believe there

is any kind of fiscal responsibility within government today will continue to view the stewardship of government funds by government officials and their bureaucratic minions in a most negative manner. We will continue to be less than happy with fiscal policy and those elected and employed people responsible for that policy.

It would seem to me that, other than the most liberal of liberals who still believe that the answer to any and all problems is to be found in government, the rest of us can hardly stand the waste, inefficiency, and stupidity of governmental bureaucracy.

Given that approximately one-third of the revenue collected evaporates due to inefficient and wasteful government programs and bureaucracy, it's hard to convince taxpaying citizens that the answer to all of our problems is to raise taxes and expand government. History, time and again, has proven that raising taxes will only increase the size of government, not improve government's efficiency. It is time that citizens act in a mature and realistic manner to at long last admit this age-old fact.

At any rate, remove politics from the taxation equation. Make it fair, simple, and understandable for all.

An equal tax based on percentage will work for everyone. This is pure equality, justice, and fairness for all. An equal percentage for all even aligns itself well with those

The Citizens Initiative Party

with an absolutely leftist agenda, such as Communist or Socialist. Everyone is treated equally. (But I doubt they'd agree; they don't like to agree with anything.)

= (Equal) Taxation

IX. Magicians

We've all enjoyed watching clever magicians. The illusions created by these folks capture our attention as we watch them perform their magic. But in the back of our minds, we know the truth. We are being fooled by these entertainers. Yet we come away from their performance asking, "How did he do that?"

We are **distracted** is the answer. Our eyes and our mind are ***focused elsewhere***, away from where the sleight of hand is going on. At the moment we are distracted, the deception occurs. We are not focused on what is really happening, even as it occurs right in front of our eyes. As a result, we don't see the reality, only what the magician wants us to see.

But while magicians are great deceivers and marvelous illusionists, there is another group that can make professional magicians look like beginners. These individuals are masters at creating illusions and deceptions, focusing our attention away from what is really going on. Of course, I'm speaking about our elected officials at all levels.

The Citizens Initiative Party

Even the most casual perusal of any recent legislation on the national or state levels (and I don't care what state you reside in) will reveal that legislative bills contain so many riders or add-ons or amendments that no one has any idea of what legislation was just passed on the legislative floor. This is real sleight of hand.

For example, a transportation bill may well contain language that legalizes medicinal marijuana or some other strange thing having absolutely nothing to do with transportation. Who knows? This sort of strange, non-bill language is always hidden in the voluminous pages of legislation. And of course, the politician, having limited time, reads the bill only thoroughly enough to find that **the one portion of the bill he is interested in is included in the document.**

Unfortunately, due to time limitations, bills are rarely read in their entirety. When the vote on the bill is taken, politicians vote for or against said bill with no regard for the other stuff in the legislation **s**o long as **their "stuff"** is in the final package. The illusion continues.

And so it goes. This has been going on for years. Although it has been a while since there has been one, can you imagine being a politician voting on a budget that is so voluminous that it has to be wheeled to your office on a handcart? And, usually, based on past practice, budget bills are wheeled to the elected official's office on the evening just prior to the day the vote on the budget is to be taken. How could these elected officials possibly know what they are voting on?

Maybe you need to enjoy politics to understand this political madness. Or maybe you just need to enjoy being deceived. Unfortunately, during every political campaign there are always the allegations of impropriety on the part of every candidate because of their voting record. For instance, while the elected official may have found their "stuff" in the transportation bill, what inadvertently happened is that, along with their vote in favor of their "stuff," there was an amendment hidden within the bill calling for a revamping of some obscure entitlement program or some other unrelated legislative agenda. Then at the time of the next election process, the candidate's opponent and the press can level all sorts of charges against the candidate based on his voting record for reasons that only make sense in the political arena. As a result of this entangled legislative mess and the spin created by the press and the candidate's opponent's "handlers," voters are left to choose between the lesser of two crooks to represent them in the legislative branch of government.

So when the campaigning is over with and the press has had their way with candidates, the voting public is left believing that neither of the candidates deserves our vote. How tragic that we must choose between two soiled and tarnished candidates. Worse yet, during our national election process, the rest of the world is watching. As a result of our election process and the negative campaign ads, the world has heard so much of the "dirt" and "spin" information on candidates that far too many candidates appear to be nothing other than "lowlifes."

If during the political campaign, the opponents can't do enough damage to each other's reputation, then the media will jump into the fray to add to the carnage. All of this will practically reduce both candidates to the status of bum. Now after all of this, the winner, let's say of the presidency, must stand up as an "honorable" leader after being reduced to a slimeball during the campaign. The present style of political campaign reduces the leader of the free world to looking anything but reputable in the eyes of the world. This is MBE!

But there's a way to end this quagmire.

Legislation needs to be "stand alone." That is to say, a transportation bill would contain only transportation measures, and nothing else. A defense bill would contain only defense items, and nothing else, and so forth. A major benefit to "stand alone" legislation is that the voting public could understand this legislation and have a clear view as to how their representative voted on any given issue. It would then be easy for the voter to make a determination with regard to the quality of the job their representative is doing representing their needs. End the illusion. End the confusion. End the deception. Stop the sleight-of-hand MBE. The legislator will need to vote on the bill as it pertains to the subject matter at hand and *only* that subject matter.

In addition to stand-alone legislation, there is also a need for "sunset laws." "Sunset" means that laws, as written and passed, would be in effect only for a certain length of time. Then they would expire. If the original bill, as passed, has merit and worth and, if it is delivering the expected results in an efficient manner and for a reasonable cost, it would be re-enacted. It could be reintroduced "as is," revamped and improved, or, if ineffective, simply allowed to expire. With stand-alone legislation and sunset laws, elected officials would then vote the bill up or down based on its merits alone.

Of course there will be political hacks who find it in their best political interest to defend the now practiced purpose-driven confusion for confusion's sake. They will argue that it takes too long to set up a bill for consideration. And once a bill is set up, why not just add amendments or riders without regard for the original intention and purpose of the bill?

In addition, they will argue, no one will benefit from a revision for the purpose of clarity, so let's simply continue on with business as usual. The hacks may be correct in many of their points of view. However, they are not considering one group that really should be well-informed and clearly understand what is going on in Congress — that would be the citizens of this nation who want to vote intelligently.

Please, political hacks, don't try to argue that there would be so many legislative bills that the numbers might get confusing or run out. I am confident we won't run out of numbers right away. Remember, these are the same elected officials who have taken this nation some **$17 trillion-plus dollars** into debt and with more debt on the way. So, consequently, there are a lot of numbers for yet undeveloped legislative bills left to work with in the future.

Besides the public being made more aware of what's going on in the legislature, come campaign time, there would be no confusion as to how any given candidate has voted in the past. All any candidate would need to do at election time would be to justify his or her voting to constituents based on an easy-to-follow voting record. Simple. Clean. Righteous.

Stand-Alone Legislation with Sunset Laws

X. Untouchables

During the Prohibition Era of the 1920s and 1930s, Chicago, Illinois, was the epicenter of bootlegging (the illegal liquor business), crime, and corruption. This was mobster Al "Scarface" Capone's town. Capone was having things his own way. Payoffs to law enforcement personnel and members of the Chicago judicial system were commonplace. The bribed police force turned a blind eye on Capone's operations, and judges were bought off.

Illicit money flowed into Capone's pockets in a big way. The crime wave was so rampant and the piles of murder victim's bodies so vast that a group of Chicago businessmen pleaded with the Bureau of Prohibition of the U.S. Treasury Department to set up operations in the city to try to get the criminal activity, corruption, and murder rate under control.

Heading up the Bureau of Prohibitions enforcement arm was a man named Eliot Ness. Ness formed a group of agents who became known as the Untouchables. The press dubbed this group the Untouchables because, try

The Citizens Initiative Party

as he might, these individuals were of such high moral standards and impeccable character that they refused Capone's and other gangsters offers to be bought off. They were above accepting bribes. And in the end, Eliot Ness and his Untouchables were able to put Al Capone and others of the Chicago area's mobsters out of business.

Would it be possible for the voting public to find candidates for public office possessing the morals exemplified by the Untouchables? Could these candidates possibly remain so true to their core values that, even after elected to office, they would remain untouchable? Eliot Ness found this incorruptible type of people ninety years ago. Are there people of this level of character and integrity still in existence in this nation today who would be willing to run for office? Given what goes on politically today, this is a fair question.

Perhaps the system of tenure and seniority in elected office plays a huge role in perpetuating the travesty of corruption in politics. Apparently, once in elected office, job one is nothing other than to be re-elected. Political campaigns cost a lot of money. Because of this fact, fund raising is so important, perhaps **the most important** part of campaigning for re-election. How very sad.

Over time, our democratic process has become polluted by corruption and greed funded by various forms of bribery.

Richard L. Freitag

Because of political correctness, we don't refer to bribery as such anymore. Instead we have learned to speak of "soft money," "lobbying," "political action committees," "special interest funds," and other less sinister sounding phrases for what amounts to payoffs, bribery, and influence peddling of elected officials. We are told we should accept, tolerate, or not care that this bribery is an acceptable political practice. What MBE!

Our legislative process, along with the political parties and governmental systems controlling the election process, has been reduced to nothing more than a commodity to be bought by the highest bidder or sold or traded for the greatest price. We citizens could simply choose to ignore the bribery that is taking place if the United States of America was just another "banana republic." However, for the greatest nation on earth with the largest economy in the world, this systematized bribery perpetuated by the major political parties and their elected politicians is a national disgrace and an international embarrassment. It is a sad situation when our nation's children equate politics and politicians with crime and corruption. Elected officials should be positive role models for future generations rather than examples of crime and corruption. True leadership is accomplished by example. How very disgusting that there are politicians for sale.

Naturally, those elected officials guilty of accepting bribes will contend that this ongoing practice of systematized bribery is necessary to get things done politically. Thus, this fouled system is perpetuated without shame or remorse by those involved and is protected by allowance and the old familiar "this is how we've always done things" mentality.

Certainly, not all politicians are taking bribes. But, in one form or another, certainly most are being influenced by various bribery schemes. If these so-called public servants are "on the take," "for sale," or can be "bought for a price," how can they be considered anything other than those who practice "the world's oldest profession"? It may be that the politicians accepting bribes are worse. After all, prostitutes are only selling their bodies, while the politicians taking bribes are selling their souls, their integrity, and any semblance of morality and ethics they may ever have possessed. In the final analysis, the primary difference between those practicing the world's oldest profession and the bribed politicians is that the prostitutes are at least honest and up front about their means of enrichment.

The decisions made by elected officials regarding legislation and public law are of far too much importance in the lives of the citizenry of this country to be allowed to be diminished to the level of ***a commodity*** *to be bought and sold at market. The plain truth is that bribery, which allegedly helps with the decision making process, is systematized government corruption! Systematized bribery must be ended for good and ended right now!*

To demonstrate how bribery is ingrained in politics, government, and the election process, here is an interesting item from the IRS official taxpayers guide:

"Bribes and kickbacks to governmental officials are deductible unless the individual has been convicted of making the bribe or has entered a plea of not guilty or nolo contendere."

In 2001, a member of the Republican Party (Senator John McCain, R-AZ) in conjunction with a member of the Democratic Party (Senator Russ Feingold, D-WI) made an attempt to stop campaign finance corruption. The McCain-Feingold Campaign Finance Reform Bill, when finally passed, had little to do with the original intent of the legislation as introduced. This is the legislation that mandates candidates say at the end of their political advertisements, "I'm (insert name), and I approve this message."

Really, that's about all that's left of the original bill. In its final form, there were so few teeth left in the legislation that it needed dentures. Imagine that! A bill to put a stop to the bribery and corruption involved in campaign finance reduced to a mere shadow of its original intent. Nice try, guys!

This weakened final form of the original bill that passed through the legislative process is a perfect example of the pathetic results achieved when working through an entrenched system of government corruption. Sadly, this system of corruption will not be abolished by members of either major political party. There is simply too much at stake for them to make this form of corruption anything other than an "honorable" practice. Only a small but determined group of "untouchables" (not from either of the two existing major political parties) could end this national disgrace.

Besides ending bribery, there are several other things honorable people running for office should do. First, elected public servants and all political appointees should understand they are just what the title of their office states in very clear terms — *public* servants. As such, they need to understand that they live in a glass house. Their lives become *public* in every sense of the term. Therefore, there should be a law that requires individuals who wish to qualify as political candidates for public office or political appointments at all levels of government to submit for *public scrutiny* their birth certificate, all school records, military records, tax records for the past seven years, police records, college records, and any other pertinent information that could be of interest to the public. The voting public would then be completely aware of a candidate's background. No secrets hidden from the voter. (Just an idea — this could be called the **OBAMA LAW** — because we've never had more of a mystery man in the presidency.)

Second, elected public servants should realize they have a responsibility to the citizens of this nation to live a life that will serve as an example to others — a life of righteousness, integrity, and honesty. We presently have plenty of the other kind of examples. *Real leaders know that true, pure leadership can only be accomplished by example.* For instance, when cheating is practiced and condoned at the highest levels of elected public office, and when these cheaters get caught and discovered, how can it be expected that children who see these powerful individuals as role models will not think of cheating as proper behavior? This just makes practical sense. However, obviously, this is not the commonly held belief with so many who presently hold office.

Bribery, corruption, and cheating have no place in our politics and our government!

We need a new breed of politicians of Untouchable character!

XI. Political Correctness

It is politically *incorrect* these days to speak of such things as *personal responsibility, individual freedom* (or for that matter, the individual) and *self-reliance*. These ideas concerning individualism have been eclipsed by now-familiar terms such as "societal responsibility," "the public good," "the common good," "public welfare," public this, or public that. Gone is the *individual*, reduced to something of no significance or relevance whatsoever. The *individual* has been replaced by the masses in our politically correct environment. Pure MBE!

Would it be fair to say that it is *individuals* who willingly gather together to form societies? Or that "the masses" are a massed group of *individuals?* Or that it is *individuals* who contribute to the betterment of any society? If this is so, other than for the sake of political correctness, why are *individuals* no longer of any importance?.

Political correctness has made or has tried to make ***society***, rather than any individual, responsible for nearly everything — either successes or failures. (Oh, that's right, there are no failures anymore.) Because political correctness has won the day, the children of our society are being taught that everyone is a winner. No one loses — ever. There is no failure. So, we play games without keeping score because then nobody has to have their precious self-image harmed in any way. There are no punitive consequences for not doing your best. There is only the fouled notion that everybody is a winner.

The new goal, apparently, for children within the most liberal-slanted public education system, seems to be that all are made to feel equal, and mediocrity is to be esteemed. Let's all be just average. In so doing, we can all feel comfortable at the lowest common denominator. Or better yet, let's make sure everyone is made to feel they are somehow exceptional. This is always so uplifting for all. However, the truth is that when everyone is supposedly exceptional, in reality, no one is really exceptional at all.

What a pathetic lie to perpetrate on children by these mindless, liberal, babying, coddling, politically correct do-gooders. Perhaps the purpose of this do-gooder mind-set is to delay the truth and to forgo an explanation of the dynamics of the ***real*** world. Should society wait to reveal the truth to these young adults until the time they graduate from high school? Or, better yet, wait with the truth until young adults are 21 or even 30 years of age? Maybe at that same time too, do-gooders could let these young people in on the truth about Santa Claus, the Easter Bunny, and the Tooth Fairy. (Hope this didn't ruin these secrets for some.) What MBE!

Another fine example of political correctness is demonstrated when the do-gooders mislead children about decision making. Fear of making a choice or a decision has become the accepted norm in our educational system. Children are taught that making a choice or a decision might upset someone, cause hard feelings, or damage someone's self-image. It has become inappropriate to make decisions or take a stand or make a choice. What if there are **consequences? YIKES!** In reality, public education is creating children who are completely and totally dependent, spineless **wimps!**

But what if we dropped political correctness and children were taught that decision making goes hand in hand with consequences? And what if they were to learn that consequences are not always about punishment? What if children were taught that the word consequence, in truth, is a synonym of "result"? What if children were taught that any decision or failure to make a decision, any choice or failure to make a choice, any stance or failure to take a stance will result in a consequence no matter what? Therefore, consequences will result in either rewards, neutrals, or punishments. This could start something! What if children were taught that it's okay to fail, provided that a much-needed lesson is learned and, in the process, that nobody gets injured?

Children should be taught the concept that failure is not negative if learning takes place. They should be taught that decision making is an exciting challenge. In that regard, children should be taught a lesson about one of America's greatest companies — 3M — which does all sorts of research on a daily basis. The results of all experimentation are kept on file. Their corporate attitude is that they never have failures — only learning experiences. And think of the wonderful products this great company has brought to market for the betterment of us all, despite what the politically correct may view as experimental failures.

When political correctness is exposed for the phoniness and waste and MBE it really is, perhaps then the *individual* will once again really count. But those of the politically correct mind-set equate individualism with selfishness. When the idea of individual worth or the concept of individual responsibility is brought up, those who cannot deal with reality always inform those who do not share their viewpoint that they (those comfortable with individualism) are greedy. Those who do not share the politically correct viewpoint concerning the public good, for example, are viewed by the politically correct as self-serving or not open minded to the needs of others. The **non-politically** correct, who enjoy the status of being an individual, are then conveniently termed **selfish** by the politically correct masses who are incapable of thinking for themselves.

But, let's take a look at true selfishness. In truth, it's not the non-politically correct that are selfish, but the other way around. How can it be that imposing one's problems on someone other than oneself is anything but selfish? ***Isn't it completely and totally selfish when your problems are forcibly made to be my problems?*** Your problems are my problems only by personal choice ***on my part.*** But what if I don't wish to deal with your problems? What if I believe that it should be *you* who deals with the problems you have made for yourself? Again, this is such MBE!

In the twisted world of political correctness, if it is acceptable for others to make their problems my problems, is it then acceptable for me to make my problems other people's problems in a likewise fashion? Or, in the world of political correctness, should responsible people be punished for making responsible choices? Would it be acceptable for me to go on a reckless spending spree without regard for my ability to pay back the loans or pay off the credit card bills and ask or force others to pay those bills for me? To use the favorite line of those for whom reality is of no consequence in this politically correct society, *"but that's different."* (This is the favorite rebuttal of those who wish to remain childish when logic and reason fail them and their arguments' position.)

But then, if it is okay for some people to live with complete indifference toward living in a responsible manner, why is it not okay for me to do likewise? After all, if a carefree, irresponsible lifestyle is a socially accepted, politically correct norm to be financed by society, shouldn't any problems I create for myself be taken care of in a likewise fashion? If I choose to become careless and irresponsible, shouldn't I be rewarded for my incompetence as well? Would society take care of all problems I could possibly create? Evidently, not so.

Apparently, societal problem fixes are okay for some, but not okay for others. It would seem that responsible individuals are *not* entitled to have all of their problems fixed by society because they have made the choice to live in a responsible manner. MBE!

At present, given the politically correct mentality, it would appear that responsible citizens do not fit the mold of the political correctness. Those living a responsible lifestyle are therefore being financially victimized for living that responsible lifestyle because they have made the choice to live within their means. As a result, the irresponsible are rewarded at the expense of the responsible. This is fairness? Oh yes, right, ***"but that's different."***

But what if there really is caring and concern for the well-being of others by those who choose to live responsibly? What if the responsible element within our society simply does not agree with the non-realist's do-gooder methods or thinking in this regard? What if responsible citizens believe that some tough lessons along the way in life will really be the most effective teacher of personal responsibility? What if those who choose to be irresponsible, non-thinking, or unrealistic were made to "fix their own wagon"? Many of life's best and longest-lasting lessons are the ones that result in some grief and hardship to the individual who caused his or her own problems in the first place.

To add to my observations concerning political correctness, I have witnessed that the true do-gooder dreamers in society are more concerned with "the try" than with the result. I'm a results guy. We disagree by nature.

For instance, look at government-sponsored neighborhood help projects of the past and present. How many times do we need to watch a couple of slick hustlers run off with the cash while the people who really need the help end up with nothing? *"Oh, but we tried."*

How many times has this country delivered food and medical supplies to war-ravaged, dictator-run Third World countries only to have these goods sold by those in power just so they can buy more armaments and explosives? The people who needed the help get nothing because of the government or the dictator's corruption. *"Oh, but we tried."*

The citizens of the United States of America are the most generous, giving, supportive people on Earth. We have proven we will come to the aid of those in need for the last 200 years. But let us not confuse generosity with being suckers. From now on, when nations seek our help, let us make it our policy that *our* people will deliver the needed supplies of food and medicine directly to those who need the help the most. **We will deliver directly** to the people in need and not entrust this business to anyone other than our personnel. If these terms are unacceptable to the government of those in need, we will let others come to the aid of those in peril. No more ***trying.*** Helping the needy is strictly about ***doing.***

How many times has this nation sent troops to help freedom fighters or to protect the civilian population in a war-ravaged area? When our troops are deployed to help stop the bloodshed and in the midst of combat some civilians are killed, those who requested that our troops be deployed at the onset then become those screaming that our troops are guilty of wrong doing. The politically correct cannot and will not be satisfied, regardless of the situation.

So in this era of political correctness, it has been decided by those elite political correctness practitioners that *there is no longer any individual responsibility.* Criminal activity, failed public education, domestic abuse, child neglect, drug addiction, refusal to act in a personally responsible manner, and on and on, now become societal issues.

It's all about *society, not the individual.*

As a result of my most heartfelt desire to be "politically correct," I have devised a new and hopefully politically correct acronym, **MBE.** This acronym has been used several times in this book. The **"M"** stands for the "male." The **"B"** stands for "bovine," meaning "oxen" or "cows." The **"E"** stands for "excrement," meaning fecal matter or poop. So we have *male bovine excrement.*

A male bovine is a bull. So **MBE is my new acronym for BULLSHIT!**

Because it is politically incorrect to use the word "bullshit" or to utter the two letters "BS" in politically correct company, this new acronym should do the trick.

Richard L. Freitag

It is my hope that this new term is politically correct enough to please those who find political correctness to be a worthwhile endeavor.

A fair summation of political correctness would be to label all of it pure MBE!

XII. Alternative Caricature Ideas

One of the all-time iconic expressions of environmental protection is the Department of Agriculture U.S. Forest Service's Smokey the Bear. Children learn about Smokey at a very early age. The cartoon caricatures of Smokey with his Forest Service hat are cute and effective tools for teaching fire prevention responsibility to children. Kids love Smokey.

Perhaps our politically correct society accepts the concept of personal responsibility provided that a cute, fuzzy caricature is pointing out who is responsible for fire prevention. The majority of U.S. Forest Service posters show Smokey the Bear pointing an accusing finger and saying, "Only you can prevent forest fires."

Another iconic American caricature is good old Uncle Sam. Posters of Uncle Sam show the stately old gentleman in his stovepipe hat looking us directly in the eye and pointing his finger at us while saying, "I WANT **YOU** for the U.S. Army."

Richard L. Freitag

Both of these iconic American caricatures point their respective accusing fingers (which is a "no-no" in our politically correct society) and demand personal responsibility (another "no-no") from the onlooker.

Because both caricatures have been around so long, this is perhaps why the politically correct tolerate them and their messages, despite the fact that each points out personal responsibility by individuals. Smokey and Uncle Sam have been useful to government agencies for a long time. Both caricatures define a concept that is found to be disgusting and archaic by the politically correct. That concept is the antiquated idea of individuals accepting and displaying personal responsibility.

But what if these caricatures or those of a similar nature could be used by the government to convey other messages? (I don't think the U.S. Forest Service would like to loan out its mascot nor would the military recruitment services want Uncle Sam on loan either.) For instance, what if government agencies had someone or something other than Smokey who was a cute, cuddly, fuzzy creature pointing an accusing finger while saying, "Only you can prevent ..."

- *Your* drug addiction problem.
- *Your* involvement in criminal gang activities.
- *Your* stupidity when making choices or decisions.
- *Your* devil-may-care attitude.

The Citizens Initiative Party

- *Your* inability to act in a socially acceptable manner.
- *Your* inability to live within a budget.
- *Your* self-justification for quitting school.
- *Your* imprisonment.
- *Your* being a burden on society.
- Welfare fraud.
- Teen pregnancy.

Or, if we used the words of Uncle Sam, he could say, "I want you to …"

- Take responsibility for *your* own choices and actions.
- Act in an adult-like manner.
- Be a proper role model for children.
- Quit making excuses.
- Quit whining.
- Quit blaming others for *your* problems
- Quit making *your problems someone else's problems*.
- Pay *your* own bills.
- Make positive contributions to society.
- Quit believing you are "owed" anything.
- Quit feeling sorry for yourself.
- Live up to the obligations you have made.
- Understand that there is *nothing* "free" other than

the air you breathe. For everything else, there is a cost. Even if that cost is not to you, someone has to pay.
- ▶ Wake up!
- ▶ Grow up!

I don't suppose the government will be launching any of these campaigns or using any of these slogans for some time to come. After all, these notions are definitely not politically correct.

So, what is the point in this brief chapter? How about this: Be it elected officials, employed bureaucrats, or U.S. citizens in general, let's understand that it's time to:
- ▶ Quit making excuses!
- ▶ Quit whining!
- ▶ End the blame game!
- ▶ Understand you are owed nothing!
- ▶ Take personal responsibility!
- ▶ Act like an adult!
- ▶ Grow up!

XIII. Public Education Lesson

My wife is a retired elementary public school teacher. We were at a social gathering a while back in which there were several other public educators present. Some very animated conversations took place, and it was most interesting to listen. Here in Wisconsin, Governor Scott Walker and the Wisconsin Legislature took away public employee bargaining rights for all public employees except law enforcement and fire fighting personnel. There are a lot of less-than-happy public employees here in Wisconsin at the present time. This includes many public educators.

I was listening to the conversation regarding teacher salaries. Naturally, several of those present were not happy at all with their current employment situation with frozen salary caps, etc. As the conversation progressed, there was an expression of serious dislike, even hatred for the governor and the legislature. I wasn't surprised.

However, one comment gained my attention. I was surprised to hear one of the teachers defending the governor. "You know what?" he said. "Governor Walker is absolutely correct in that public education is a broken failure and needs to be revamped for the betterment of the children and the parents of this state. I feel things are so bad that I wish we could just start over." I was quite shocked by his comment.

Interestingly, the educator who made the statement and his spouse elected to send their children to a parochial school. Yes, they paid the tuition and sent their children to a privately funded school even though he earned his living working in the public education arena.

So, I asked him this question, "Can you explain the strange dichotomy between public school teacher salaries and the quality of education for the children involved in the public education system and the much lower private school teacher salaries but the higher quality of education for the children involved in the parochial education system?"

His one word answer was immediate, brilliant, and to the point, with a directness and simplicity that caused me to really think about it. I had never considered his one-word answer before. This one word could be the answer to so many of the governmental problems that this country faces beyond just public education. His one-word answer was, **"OWNERSHIP!"**

He went on to say, "I have kids in my classroom whose parents I have never met. They are completely unconcerned and uninvolved in their children's education and lives. They couldn't care less. They take no ownership whatsoever in their child's education. Apparently, they do not believe they are responsible and have no interest in anything other than themselves. What am I as a teacher supposed to do? While I can care very much for and about each of the children in my classroom, I can't be every kid's parent and take parental responsibility for each and every one. I cannot be every child's parent!"

Then he went on to tell how "delighted" he is every morning to see a number of so-called parents drop off their children while sitting in their 4x4 SUVs smoking cigarettes and texting or talking on their cell phones. The children of these so-called parents qualify for free breakfast and free lunch meals supplied by the school at ***taxpayer expense.*** Evidently, 4x4 SUVs, cell phones, and cigarettes are far more important than the care and feeding of their children. Is this blatant irresponsibility and selfishness or what?

Oh, but don't worry, it isn't costing us anything — the government is paying for it. It's FREE!

Unfortunately, the real problem with the attitude and mind-set in the statement above is that there are actually people stupid enough to believe such a statement to be true! Talk about greed! Talk about self-serving convenience! Use a government program to pay for that which should be *your* responsibility and, more importantly, one of the highest priorities for any parent — the care and feeding of *your* children. How can anyone other than the most self-centered, greedy, looking-for-a-handout person justify smoking $7 per package cigarettes, paying cell phone fees, and making SUV payments while having their children fed at taxpayer expense? Isn't this greed? How is making other people pay for your responsibilities while you waste money on other items anything other than the most self-serving greed at the highest level? Here again we have a case of forcing other people to take responsibility for that which should be *your* responsibility alone. This is truly nothing other than self-serving greed on steroids.

Parents of children in parochial schools take "ownership" in their child's education. They have a vested interest in the school. These parents are involved in their child's school and for good reason. In a way, the parochial school belongs to them. Those paying for a premium education for their children believe they must take ownership in the school. Therefore, they know what is going on in the classroom. It is in their best interest to know the teacher, the curriculum, how their child is performing in the classroom environment and so forth. These taxpaying parents pay for the cost of public education through taxation, and yet, at the same time they willingly pay tuition for the parochial education for their children.

Ownership

Taking the concept of ownership a step further, could this simple idea of taking ownership be of benefit in other areas of government operations as well?

Consider this. The majority of present day "entitlement programs" are operated and funded based on mandates at the state or the national level. In so doing, a separation or disconnect is created between the government agency provider of the funding and the goods or services and the recipients of the assistance. It all becomes so sterile, so non-personal, so distant. These programs are run by government bureaucrats who deem their particular government program to be a *success* for their agency or department if there is an *increase in the number of people being served by their agency.* Yes, this is the bureaucratic mind-set. This is *success?*

Reality, practicality, and sound judgment need to come into play with regard to entitlement programs. Success should be viewed in terms of a *decrease* in the number of people being served. The situation we currently find ourselves in is because these programs are left in the hands of bureaucrats who need to *increase* numbers of people being served in their programs to justify their budget and their employment. Bureaucrats build fiefdoms.

But how did the citizens of this nation allow this disconnect between local operations and state and national government-funded programs to happen? Is it apathy? Is it laziness? Is it convenience? Is it irresponsibility? Or, how about all of the above?

Review this selection of questions and see if you agree that things could be made better, simpler, and more effective for everyone by making these simplistic "ownership" changes to government operations.

- ▶ What if *local* area residents were to serve on *local* boards to give oversight to *local* government programs?
- ▶ What if *local* citizens held the purse strings for *local* operations?
- ▶ What if there was a *local* personal relationship with individuals involved in government-funded entitlement programs of all sorts?
- ▶ What if, instead of continuing with the mindless status quo, *local* board members said to those seeking help, "Here are five posted jobs in the area. You need to go get one," instead of

simply handing out funds with few if any strings attached?
- What if many of the federal and state funded programs were brought back to the *local* level for both funding and operation?
- In my example of the money-hungry corrupt local official from Chapter VIII, how long would such a person last if subjected to *local* oversight and the concept of *local* ownership on a daily basis?

Of course there is a problem here. Currently, government officials and bureaucrats believe they can excuse themselves from taking responsibility for any and all government-sponsored programs. They simply need to tell the public how much funding they have allocated to these various government programs. We have all heard responses like, "Well, we've spent X millions on this. What more do you want from us?"

A good response to the elected official giving an answer like the one above would be, "As a matter of fact, Senator, I want to know what was achieved for the funds that were spent. What good did this program really do for the people who needed the help? How has this nation been made a better place because of the money spent? Was this an improvement in the lives of those targeted for the program, or was this just another situation where well-intentioned ideas and funds ended up in the hands of a few slick hustlers? Would you care to comment, Senator? But please, answer the questions in a direct manner."

Again, I have personal experience with this. When I was the Commander of my VFW Post, a person claiming to be a veteran asked us for help. According to his story, he and his five children were living in a pickup truck camper, and he needed $150.

Our post member who was initially approached by this individual knew there was something phony about his story when the requester couldn't even spell Vietnam properly while claiming to be a veteran of that war. He spoke of cities and areas in Korea, not Vietnam. Not one of the Post members ever saw the children. Despite the questions about who we were dealing with, our contacted post member provided this "veteran" with seven "Help Wanted" ads from the local paper. He even offered two personal contacts wherein he knew the local companies were looking for workmen. This "veteran" made no effort to contact any of the leads (because we checked) and insisted instead on speaking to our general membership. So we let him.

It was soon obvious that we were dealing with a panhandler. All he could do was offer up excuses as to why he couldn't be bothered to seek employment. His request for funds was "tabled." Had we simply given this imposter the funds he requested, there would be that much less funding available for **real** veterans and their families who have **real** needs. There is no funding or program that has unlimited sources available.

My VFW Post, along with all veterans' organizations across the country, has helped countless veterans and their families on innumerable occasions. We will always come to the assistance of any fellow veteran and family with few, if any, questions. It's not too difficult to figure out who is and who is not a real veteran. Real veterans can all "talk the talk." We have a program in place within our local post, as well as programs at the regional and national levels with quite a substantial pool of funding available to assist veterans and their families in time of need. We regard any veteran as our brother or sister and treat them accordingly with respect, dignity, and an outpouring of help and assistance — whatever the need may be.

But not panhandlers and phonies and bums who believe it's their right to milk the system seeking a handout!

I use this example to point out that local "ownership" could eliminate government waste and expose those who wish to abuse public assistance. In the case I shared, we had a direct connection to the person in question. By our personal involvement in this case, and our review and oversight of our own funds, we were able to expose this so-called "veteran" as one who was seeking a free ride.

Americans are the most generous people in the world. We will always help those in need. However, help and assistance should be temporary for those of fit mind and body. Help should not define a lifestyle, nor should being publicly assisted define a career.

Now, let's take this "ownership" argument a bit further. What is the purpose of the *federal* departments of education, commerce, housing, and energy? Talk about wasteful, bureaucratic government funding! What do these federal departments do that couldn't be better handled locally to make a positive impact on the local community? How do these departments of the federal government make the United States of America a better place in which to live and in which to raise and educate tomorrow's citizens?

For instance, wouldn't education be better served if running schools was a completely *local* issue? Neither bureaucrats in the state education departments nor those at the federal level in Washington, D.C., can fix what is wrong in individual local schools. Government bureaucrats are good at issuing unfunded edicts mandating programs that may or may not be in the best interest of the local community and local students. These distant pencil-pushers are too far removed from local problems to make positive changes or create realistic solutions. So, it's up to the *local* people. *Local* concerned citizens need to make the *local* changes — not government bureaucrats in some far-off place issuing edicts. For instance, citizens who live in Wisconsin cannot fix what is wrong with education in Idaho or Alabama or any other state. And those in Washington, D.C., can't do any better. But local people can make positive and timely *local changes within their local community.*

Think of the educational opportunities children would have if their local school district was allowed to locally allocate all funding rather than sending tax dollars to state or federal collection agencies first. Gone would be the government grants for education. Communities would be able to provide the best education for *their* children, set *their* standards for *their* children, remedy problems for *their* children and not be bound by state and federal mandates. Local schools would become a source of community pride, setting or even raising the bar for other school districts around them.

Wasted funding for any and all government programs is such a sad story. One-third of the money paid into the government is lost to inefficiency and bureaucracy before any funds can be returned to the local community to fund local programs through grants. To simplify this, *state or national governments cannot provide funding to any local entity without first confiscating those funds from the local populace. There are no "free" funds available. Again, all government funds are first confiscated from citizens before they can be returned to local communities — that is, returned to the local communities less the waste and inefficiency of government bureaucracy. What a tragedy!*

Keep local funds local so that wasteful government bureaucracy on both state and national levels is eliminated.

In light of what I've just shared, here is another list of questions for you to consider:
- ▶ What if there was a review of federal and state government entities and many of these were eliminated in favor of local government entities?
- ▶ What if both control and funding of a number of national and state government programs reverted to local government?
- ▶ What would happen to local government budgets, local oversight, and local responsibility should state and national government confiscation be ended?

- ▶ Isn't it true that federal and state government funding or grants at the local level would be impossible without prior confiscation in the first place?
- ▶ Could the elimination of state and national bureaucratic waste result in more available funding for local government entities?

The point of this chapter is that many aspects of government need to be placed ***back in the hands of the local populace.*** As a nation, if the problems we face are to be repaired, we will need:

- ▶ Local control.
- ▶ Local oversight.
- ▶ Local involvement.
- ▶ Local "ownership."

We need to place government in the hands of local people who can actually take corrective actions as the need arises and in a timely fashion.

XIV. Formation, Objectives, and Organization of the Party

Just to clarify, with the exception of my career and background information, all of the thoughts and ideas in this book are offered for your consideration for the express purpose of organizing, activating, and operating a third major, permanent political party. Therefore, it is my proposal that there be established the Citizens Initiative Party. The visionary goal of the Citizens Initiative Party is to become a long-term, major presence on the American political landscape. Ours will not be a "party of one" formed for a one-time run at the presidency.

The Citizens Initiative Party will *not* be just another organization intent on perpetuating systematized government corruption and waste. Rather our intention is *to end it!*

The Citizens Initiative Party

The Citizens Initiative Party will have a number of factors in its favor with regard to creating interest in the movement and the philosophy. This, in turn, will aid in the recruitment of new members. These favorable factors are as follows:

- ▶ Since the Citizens Initiative Party is to be a brand new political party and we are organizing to *reject* a number of the systematized practices of the existing parties, our newness, our fresh ideas, and our visionary approach to old, tired, worn-out past practices will create excitement within the voting public.
- ▶ The Citizens Initiative Party will be a gathering place for those who believe or know for certain that they have *no* legislative representation, *no* voice in government. The Citizens Initiative Party will be the new home for those who seek a reasonable, practical, realistic approach to government, rather than the foolishness and corruption that we despise.
- ▶ Citizens Initiative Party members and office seekers will be energetic proponents of our revisionist version of how government can and should work in the best interests of and for the maximum number of citizens.
- ▶ Members of the Citizens Initiative Party will *seek*

Richard L. Freitag

information regarding RESULTS of government expenditures, rather than being satisfied with simply an expenditure report. It will be our position that the spending of money is nothing more than a diversionary tactic by slippery politicians if we have *no definitive RESULTS to analyze, scrutinize, and review.*

- Because the two major existing parties seem satisfied to justify their government-funded programs based on excuses about how much money was spent on these wasteful programs, it should be no problem for Citizens Initiative Party candidates for public office to confront major party candidates during elections. By asking Republicans and Democrats to explain what (if anything) was accomplished by these vast government expenditures, rather than how much of the government's funding has been wasted, it will be simple to expose both parties for the frauds that they are.
- American citizens, tired of the mudslinging style of political campaigning, will respond favorably to our clean campaign practices.

The Citizens Initiative Party will attract like-minded citizens to become members in our newly formed party. These new members will, in turn, spread the positive word regarding our new party. They must let others know of our goals and objectives, of our vision for the future. We will need to define the means and methods by which we plan to achieve these goals.

Compared to political parties organized in the past, it will be much easier to form a new major political party today. The variety of technology alone will make this a far simpler job. We will set up a website that will facilitate communication through technology. This communications technology will be our initial and primary tool for promoting awareness of the existence of the Citizens Initiative Party. Through this medium primarily, an understanding of our political vision and direction will take place.

Much of the organizational work can be accomplished by telephone, fax, e-mail, Twitter and Facebook. While direct personal contact will remain a part of the formula, much of the early stages of setup for the party can be accomplished without person-to-person contact.

As membership numbers increase, local, county, and state chapters of the Citizens Initiative Party will need to be organized. The Citizens Initiative Party membership will understand that we will need political operatives at all levels of government. Without multi-layered activity on the part of the Citizens Initiative Party, we know we can have no long-term effect on the American political process. Without the various tiers of political involvement, we understand that we too will end up on that list of parties that were here today and gone tomorrow, or of a most limited political effect.

Each state, along with each county or metropolitan area in densely populated areas, will form a local party organization. Party officials at each level will need to be elected after the initial gathering. Local and regional offices as well as state and a national office will need to be established. National and state meetings will be held once a year (more often, if necessary), with delegates attending from each of the various local party organizations.

The Citizens Initiative Party National Office should be set up in a geographically central area of the country and away from the national capital. Perhaps Lincoln, Nebraska, or Jefferson City, Missouri, would work. Both cities have presidential name connections while being distant from the national capital. By establishing our national party headquarters away from the national capital's political cesspool of corruption, we will be able to keep our party operations cleaner and less apt to be influenced by money, greed, and corruption. That being said, as our party becomes viable and operational, there will most likely be a need for an office in Washington, D.C. However, under no circumstances should this office ever become our national party headquarters.

The Citizens Initiative Party

The same idea holds true for state party headquarters. They should *never* be located in state capitals. The location of state and national headquarters must be kept away from the polluted, contaminated environment we wish to change for the better.

By doing so, we will accomplish several things. First, our top party officials at the state and national levels will be removed from easy access by those purveyors of the bribery and corruption that we want ended. Second, party leadership can have a clearer, cleaner view of those political situations that we believe are in need of improvement and cleansing. You can't see things as clearly when you're in the middle of the fight as you can when you are a fight spectator. Third, office space rental costs in areas not fouled by political activity will be lower, so that our costs of operation will be kept to a minimum.

The Citizens Initiative Party will issue plastic membership cards and pins to paying members. A monthly newsletter will keep our membership informed of party activities and scheduled events. In addition to membership applications, those interested in a genuine major national third party can communicate directly with one another via social media or through the party website. The office and the website will serve as the national clearing house for the party and serve as a central coordination center for all of our party activities on national, state, and local levels. Our office will be staffed by professionals who will effectively schedule, monitor, and review organizational meetings, events, and other pertinent party business.

    The Citizens Initiative Party will establish a party platform consisting initially of no more than five planks. We will gather locally to establish issues of national interest that have a local flavor. The local chapter and then state-level meetings will be followed by our national meeting where, using local input, we will establish a simple, easily understood national party platform. We will choose no more than five issues and establish a rational, responsible approach to these issues as we see fit. By keeping our party platform and our position on these issues clear and simple, we will **not** follow the examples of the two existing major parties. The Citizens Initiative Party will **not** attempt to be "all things to all people." Instead, the Citizens Initiative Party will take a solid, clear, concise stand on our selected party platform issues. Meanwhile, the two existing major parties, because of the complexity of their platforms and their unending need to be loved by all, will continue to actually stand for nothing at all while claiming to represent the best interests of the people. Conscientious citizens will see through this worn-out smoke screen and know that these parties are

The Citizens Initiative Party

not serious about any of the real issues confronting the citizens, because their platforms are nebulous at best.

As our platform issues are resolved in our favor, we will establish new platform planks that our membership believes are in the best interest of our nation, our states, our counties, our communities. But always, we will keep our party platform clean and simple. While our platform will have but few planks, these planks will be solid. Our nation, our states, our counties, and our community's citizens will always be able to understand the platform, the planks, the position, and the agenda of the Citizens Initiative Party.

Understand that when we try to become a newly registered political party, our members and especially our party leadership will be stonewalled at every possible opportunity by election officials and bureaucrats who are very happy with the status quo. We will not be made to feel welcome. However, our perseverance will win out over those who would prefer that we did not exist.

If the Citizens Initiative Party puts forth a clear, concise, and worthwhile message, and if our vision of the future and our plan of action meet the needs of the populace with an inspired program of implementation for success, political apathy will be diminished in this nation. At such time as the citizens become politically involved once again, political corruption will be ended because those involved in various scams will come to know and understand that they are being watched for a change and must answer for their actions.

As the message of the Citizens Initiative Party becomes more widely known and is understood to be of a new and visionary concept, previously apathetic, non-voting citizens will begin to participate in, at the very least, voting. Voting is, after all, the act of responsible citizens. Voting and voter participation in the election process wield the power to effect change. At long last, the Citizens Initiative Party will offer the citizenship of this nation something and someone *to vote FOR.*

This party will:
- ▶ **Reject existing corrupt practices.**
- ▶ **Have realistic and attainable goals.**
- ▶ **Give citizens a voice in government.**
- ▶ **Offer new faces and ideas to vote for.**
- ▶ **Promote a results-oriented government.**
- ▶ **Insist on an overview and realistic analysis of government expenditures.**

All of this will cause a revolution at the ballot box!

XV. Operations and Policies of the Party

Early Operations

Once the party chapters are organized, the first order of business will be to register the party as a legal political entity. After following the steps necessary to complete this process, the Citizens Initiative Party will be eligible to place candidates' names on election ballots.

Each local chapter will need to select delegates for a state-level general membership meeting. At state meetings, the best ideas from the local chapters can be discussed and adopted. Eventually a national meeting will need to be held. Then, at the national meeting, the best ideas from the various state meetings can be discussed and adopted. At all of these meetings, we will need to discuss and then draft the bylaws and operational procedures for the party, all of which will come from the lower-level meetings of the local party chapters. In the case of the Citizens Initiative Party, citizens will actually, once again, have something to say. To make certain that our new organization is viable, legal counsel will be required to ensure the legality of our proceedings at these organizational meetings.

Citizens Initiative Party Candidates

At such time as the Citizens Initiative Party is a fully legal political party, the party will need to run candidates for public office under its banner as soon as possible. It will not be wise to seek top leadership positions until we have established our party members in city councils, county boards, and state and national legislatures. We will *not* seek top political leadership positions for our candidates until we have established some friendly faces in the legislative arena. As previously established with Governor Ventura's example, without party members in the legislative branch of government, we can expect nothing other than failure for our party members who are elected to top leadership positions. We will *not* subject our party members to the humiliation of an unbacked, unsupported top leadership position. Until such time as we have the momentum and the track record to elect party members to the legislative branches of government who would support our candidate in the top leadership position, we will not run candidates for these top-level executive positions.

Funding

If it is indeed worthwhile to be a member of the Citizens Initiative Party, members will need to understand that membership will be worth paying for. In order for the Citizens Initiative Party to be able to promote and maintain the "high road" with regard to ethics, morals, general decency, and integrity, we are duty bound to fund our operations strictly through membership dues and purely anonymous donations. Thus our membership dues may need to be slightly higher than the dues of the other parties, lest we too fall into the compromised, corrupted positions that the two major parties presently find themselves in.

We refuse to be beholding to various special interest groups and heavyweight contributors. The Citizens Initiative Party can accept *no* contributions from special interest groups or individuals with agendas they wish to promote through influence peddling and bribery. Any contribution made to the party will need to be made in a strictly anonymous manner. There can be no strings attached to any contribution made to the Citizens Initiative Party. The Citizens Initiative Party cannot be "for sale."

Richard L. Freitag

Political Campaign Operations

H. Ross Perot set the example the Citizens Initiative Party should follow with regard to how to run a political campaign. Perot demonstrated how to run a frugal campaign during his 1992 run for the presidency. Perot didn't have a huge motor coach or an airliner adorned with his picture, name, and logo. He wasn't constantly surrounded by an entourage. He never had more than three or four people accompany him on the campaign trail. Mr. Perot was not above driving a rented sedan or his own car or flying on commercial flights. **Mr. Perot was the frugal campaigner.** Practical, responsible, realistic citizens will appreciate the frugal, low-budget campaign practice of the Citizens Initiative Party.

As Citizens Initiative Party members, we must ask ourselves if all is well with America when several billion dollars are spent nationwide on political campaigns. And to what end? Could those same billions of dollars be put to better use if spent on education, health care, medical or scientific research, food and shelter for those in need, public works refurbishments, infrastructure improvements, or a host of other worthwhile endeavors?

Who, if anyone, is so mindless as to change their political views based on the hopelessly boring and repetitious political campaign advertisements we are subjected to in the various media outlets? Are there American citizens foolish enough to be swayed in their convictions by a recorded political telephone message? Is it possible that a real message of vision and credibility could be more important than the endless repetition of media promotions? Or is it true that the simple repetition of a media blitz is sufficient to overcome the lack of credibility of the less-than-forthright candidate? Think of the wasted funds!

Party Campaign Policies — The High Road

Every Citizens Initiative Party member elected to public office will be subjected to all of the bribery and corruption tactics that we, as a political party, want brought to an end. Our party members who become elected public officials will need to document all bribery attempts so that the purveyors of these corrupt practices can be exposed to the public. Although it will be a difficult task to resist the temptation to accept the bribes, Citizens Initiative Party members will need to steel themselves to the party's position with regard to integrity, honesty, decency, and character. The slightest failure to maintain the high standards of behavior established by party policy will bring embarrassment and humiliation on the party, the membership, and the individual who lets down his or her guard. Though accepted as common practice today, Citizen Initiative Party members must reject bribery and influence peddling, and this will take superhuman effort on their part. Elected Citizens Initiative Party members must raise the standard of acceptable moral and ethical behavior by setting the example for all other politicians.

Initially, when Citizens Initiative Party members are elected to public office, these folks will need to learn how "to play the game" within the confines of the legislative process. This will mean that many of the political and governmental procedures and systems we wish to end will need to be "worked with" in the long-term interest of serving the constituents these party members were elected to serve. So, at first, Citizens Initiative Party elected officials, despite detesting the systems we wish to do away with, will need to "play ball" with those who want the present systems perpetuated. This will require tremendous personal discipline and some very high-level political operations. These first elected members of the party will have the toughest job imaginable. Yet these first few elected party members will have to do the most important work in terms of the long-term goals of the party and its membership.

Citizens Initiative Party candidates for elected office will propose a political agenda for the voters' acceptance or rejection based solely on content and merit. If these objectives make sense and have validity, voters will choose to vote for the Citizens Initiative Party candidate. If the objectives make no sense and lack validity, voters will choose to have others represent them.

The Citizens Initiative Party will take the position that elections are strictly about differences of opinion and philosophy. Our party's candidates for office will not resort to personal attacks on their opposition. The political campaign tactics of the Citizens Initiative Party will raise the bar with regard to the political campaigning practices presently justified by the two major political parties. The Citizens Initiative Party will **not** lower itself to the levels of smear tactics, dirt-digging, mud-slinging and negativism that have become the norm in the current political arena. If our message is strong enough, if our ideas and principles are clear enough, if our enthusiasm is contagious enough and if our objectives are worthwhile enough, the Citizens Initiative Party and its candidates for public office **will not** want or need to resort to negativism or character assassination in its political campaigning.

Our candidates for office will not comment on other candidates' political positions or objectives. They will speak solely about their own. The public will decide what makes the most sense and will vote accordingly.

The Citizens Initiative Party will rise above the

stench of the two major political parties' campaign practices. We will take the "high road" that Americans long for. American citizens are sick of the foulness and negativity found in present-day political campaigns. Instead of trying to distract the voters from the real issues of the day by criticizing the opposition personally, our party's candidates will dwell on the positives of our platform and our political positions. Our party's candidates will focus on the true issues facing our states and our nation today. In so doing, the Citizens Initiative Party will set a new standard by raising the bar for conducting political campaigns in the United States of America.

The Citizens Initiative Party will stay out of the current campaign circus. We will conduct our campaigns on a low-budget basis — a decision that will be respected by the citizens whom we wish to attract for membership in the party. There are plenty of citizens who find the lavish spending of the major parties and their candidates to be extravagant, unjustifiable, and just plain wasteful. We can use this wastefulness of the other two parties to our advantage.

Our party's message will be:
- *Clear!*
- *Clean!*
- *Simple!*

XVI. Membership in the Citizens Initiative Party

Many of the signers of the Declaration of Independence went on to become the warriors who made possible the founding of this great nation. Those who fought to bring about this great political experiment had had enough of armed conflict when the war for independence was brought to a successful conclusion. As a result, when it came time to write the document upon which, by which, and through which this nation is governed — the Constitution of the United States of America — these early leaders made provision for change within government without war. They made provision for modification of this document **all within the limits of the Constitution and without the need to resort to violence and armed conflict to make such modification**.

Unfortunately, there are those in our nation today

who advocate government change by armed insurrection. A number of these splinter groups — primarily outlaws, crackpots, and the mentally deranged — operate throughout these United States. Besides the other problems they have, apparently these individuals are illiterate. If they were able to read and understand the history of our nation and our Constitution, they would soon come to realize that provision for change in a non-violent manner within our government is already a matter of record. Those interested in conflict should come to realize that the real battlefield for positive political change in the United States of America lies not in the streets but in the hearts and minds of a politically motivated populace.

Even the great visionaries of the past — our founding fathers — advocated change as the need arose. Thomas Jefferson said, "A little rebellion now and then is a good thing, as necessary in the political world as storms in the physical." George Washington said in this regard, "The happiness of nations can be accomplished by pacific revolutions in their political systems without the destructive intervention of the sword." Change can be accomplished in this nation without armed conflict if we are smart enough to read and heed what our founding fathers wrote in the Constitution so long ago.

The Citizens Initiative Party does not want people

who believe that violence is the only way to bring about political change as part of its membership. Our membership must recognize that our fight is a war against political apathy and that our battle plan is to bring political indifference to an end by creating a new vision and a new direction for American politics. ***The Citizens Initiative Party does not seek members from the "lunatic fringe"!***

Currently, both of the existing major political parties seem to have the political answers for many members of our society. Too many citizens seem satisfied to adopt the political position of the major parties carte blanche. These mindless individuals question nothing. Life is simple. Their political position mirrors that of their party. They don't have a need nor a desire to think. They don't even need to look at the issues. The party has taken care of that for them.

The Citizens Initiative Party will be of no use to people who are incapable of thinking. The Citizens Initiative Party is not looking for mindless robots to fill its membership rolls.

Instead, the Citizens Initiative Party membership will be made up of those who are not satisfied with the political positions and actions of either of the existing major political parties. Citizens Initiative Party members will be thinkers and visionaries who want to right the wrongs of ongoing, fouled governmental systems.

In addition, our party members will be those who have the courage not only to speak up, but to stand up for what they believe they can change for the better. Our party will be filled with activists for positive change.

The Citizens Initiative Party will seek to enlist for membership those who believe in high moral standards and ethics. Our members will believe in and abide by the idea of leadership by example. The Citizens Initiative Party will need members of "untouchable" character if it is to make the positive changes within government which its members envision and believe to be necessary.

The membership of the Citizens Initiative Party will view a lack of political experience as a *positive trait* for those members who seek elected office. Those who don't know "the system" are far more likely to bring about positive change than those who feel very comfortable while continuing to operate within the present system.

The avoidance of political entrapment by special interest groups and purveyors of "soft money" will be as difficult an assignment as could be asked of any mortal. However, there are "untouchables" within our society who are equal to the task, and they need to become Citizens Initiative Party members. These party members are the ones we will need to become our elected officials in order that the positive change we envision can progress.

The Citizens Initiative Party

These elected Citizens Initiative Party members will need to publicly expose any and all bribery attempts by those who make this illicit practice their habit. Only those of the highest moral character and virtue can possibly effect any positive change within our presently fouled government systems.

Realistically, there will be those party members, once elected, who will succumb to bribery. They will be caught up in the web of corruption. When it is discovered by fellow members of the party that these individuals are accepting bribes or other forms of graft and corruption, once caught, these members will be expelled from the Citizens Initiative Party immediately. These former members will then be free to join either of the major parties. There, they will be made to feel right at home with either their new right wing or left wing friends. After all, birds of a feather flock together.

As members of the Citizens Initiative Party, we will need to set the example for the generations to come. It is we who will need to raise the standards of political office holders by eliminating the corruption that our nation's children presently equate with politicians in general. Citizens Initiative Party members, acting in a reasonable, responsible, and adult-like manner, will need to understand that public figures "live in glass houses." We can only effect positive change by carefully considering how our speech and our actions will be perceived by the general public. We will need to lead by setting the proper example and be guided by one very simple question with regard to proper words and deeds and behavior. That simple question is: **What sort of example am I setting for future generations?** Just think of how different our political environment and our governmental systems might be had our past and present day elected officials asked themselves this very simple question!

Citizens Initiative Party members will police their fellow party members with regard to proper behavior, speech, and actions. This self-policing effort will result in in-house discipline of fellow members of the party who may have "slipped." The result of this initiative by our party membership will be that of projecting a positive party image with regard to both the present and the future direction of our party, thus ensuring a steady increase in membership.

Our membership will know and understand that the positive change we seek in government can only be made to happen through vigorous political activity and commitment. A results-oriented political platform, along with a plan to implement such a platform, will spur the general population to end the existing apathy and become politically involved. Involvement, not apathy, is needed to bring about change.

The Citizens Initiative Party

To sum up, members of the Citizens Initiative Party will be made up of the following:
- ▶ Citizens who are unsatisfied with the political status quo.
- ▶ Citizens who want to be politically proactive.
- ▶ "Untouchables" — citizens of high moral and ethical standards.
- ▶ Thinkers and visionaries.
- ▶ Citizens of a nonviolent nature and certainly *not* those of the "lunatic fringe."
- ▶ Citizens who understand that there can only be leadership by example.
- ▶ Citizens who seek positive political and governmental change.

XVII. Political Platform of the Citizens Initiative Party

The solidarity of our members' positions will result in a party unified by common goals and ideals. All Citizens Initiative Party members and elected party officials will follow the same identical party line with regard to party policy and positions, regardless of personal opinion or agenda. The Citizens Initiative Party will present to the public a political party with a clear, clean political platform. In so doing, The Citizens Initiative Party will show that it knows where it is headed, knows what it wants to accomplish, and knows how to make it happen.

Term Limits

The system of tenured office must be brought to an end. Stagnation, stalemate, and general government inaction are the result of the continuation of the system of tenured office. A regular rotation of elected officials will place in the government, at all levels, officials who are politically motivated and inspired. It will be the position of the Citizens Initiative Party that all elected government officials will be bound by term limits. The president is already restricted to eight years in office. Senators, both federal and state, may serve no more than two six-year terms in office. Representatives, both federal and state, may serve no more than six two-year terms in office. All judges may serve no more than twelve years as well.

With the enactment of term limits, officials will need to become aggressively proactive during their limited time in office. They will be restricted in time to serve their constituency. They will only be given a possible twelve years in which to accomplish that which they believe to be their political agenda while serving the needs of their electorate.

= (Equal) Taxation

Our current tax laws are so complex and confusing that we need to have a "do-over" with regard to the future of revenue sources for this country. At present, the federal tax code is more than 70,000 pages (5.5 million words) in length. No one individual can possibly understand it all. Tax laws are a mess. Taxation should be simple enough for all to understand.

The Declaration of Independence states, "All are created equal." Good enough. Then all should pay equally. The only way to accomplish this equalized taxation is to tax on a percentage basis. So, all will pay their fair share of taxes based upon an equal percentage of their income. Loopholes will be done away with completely. Gone will be the days of the politics of taxation policy. No more silly and arbitrary thresholds and no more meaningless discussion concerning ability to pay. Such discussions are nothing more than political footballs. The end to this discussion is this: if you find your ability to pay to be too difficult, it's up to you to change your economic condition — not some politicians. Therefore, all who enjoy the privileges of living in this country can and will pay the same percentage of their income. Over time, the percentage to be paid by all may vary, depending on spending by the legislature, but all will pay equally. Simple. Clean. Understandable by all.

Business entities, including all foreign-based corporations, will pay taxes to this government based upon net income generated by their operations in the United States of America. Again, no exceptions and no excuses. Any business, foreign or domestic, along with their respective executive officers, claiming to operate at a loss for more than three years (thereby avoiding the payment of taxes) will be subject to a thorough investigation and audit by the Internal Revenue Service. Punitive fines of a most severe nature will be levied against the business and its respective executive officers personally.

Stand-Alone Legislation with Sunset Laws

Legislative bills will be sent to the floor for ratification or dismissal based solely on the single purpose theme and content of the particular bill. There will be no riders, subclauses or amendments to any legislation, friendly or otherwise, which do not directly pertain to the subject matter of the original bill. So that the voting public can follow along, all legislation will stand alone on its own merits. No tricks. No gimmicks. No deception.

All legislation will be in effect for a limited time. In other words, it will have an expiration date at which time it will either need to be re-ratified or allowed to die, as the case may be. Therefore, if a given law is found to be of little positive effect, it will simply be allowed to die.

Sunset laws will result in a continual review and thorough scrutiny of all government laws on a regular basis. Review and refinement of our laws will keep the legislature honest and the public aware of the real changes that are going on in government.

Richard L. Freitag

Local Ownership of Government

It will be a goal of the Citizens Initiative Party to bring government operations and funding back to the local level as much as is possible. While there are certain governmental operations that must be handled on either the national or the state level, there are far too many government functions, along with the related funding, that need to be brought back to the local level. Citizens will be able to reclaim ownership of these government functions. As much as possible, government will be returned to the local communities.

The desired result of this idea of placing the government back in the hands of the local people has a number of positive attributes:

- ▶ By eliminating government bureaucratic waste at the national and state levels, more funding will be available for local programs. The people and programs needing the funding actually will receive more of it directly.
- ▶ Local citizens will be better able to monitor the people and programs being handled on a local basis.
- ▶ The revenue raising process will be completely simplified. Funds will go directly to the municipality, the county, or the district, rather than

going first to the state or national capital and then returned to the localities. Waste lost to bureaucracy and inefficiency within big government is eliminated.
- ▶ Fraud, corruption, stupidity, and greed will be eliminated by the fact that those employed to manage local programs will be watched very closely by those who are paying to have this local work done on their behalf.
- ▶ By placing government operations back in the hands of the local people, there will be more local involvement in government. People will realize that government is no longer a distant, nebulous, uncontrollable, unmovable object. Instead, government is about the local community, the local people, and the betterment of the local people's lives.

This is the true meaning of local "ownership" of government.

Direct Election of Candidates

As has been the case several times in our history, national candidates have been placed in office not by the choice of the people, but rather by the electoral college system. This antiquated electoral practice of the past needs to be shelved. The candidate of choice should be determined by the votes cast by the people, the so-called popular vote, not by some group of political hacks.

Trust the people. Let the people make their choice. Let them decide. Let the nation abide by the choice of the people who have voted. Let this truly be "a government of the people, by the people, and for the people."

Non-Platform Issues

Other issues facing the Citizens Initiative Party will be dealt with based on establishing a party *position* rather than adding more political platform planks. Party *positions* will be based on careful thought and consideration at all party levels. These Citizens Initiative Party *positions* will be based on the consensus of various individual local, county, and state party organizations. In so doing, we will arrive at a national party *position* to present to the voting public for their consideration on issues we do not wish to incorporate into our very simplistic national political platform.

Should the Citizens Initiative Party choose to make a political platform plank of all the issues upon which we have chosen to take a position, our platform would become similar to the political mess we are trying to do away with. We need to concentrate our efforts on a basic five-point platform, not try to be all things to all people. To put this in simple language, the Citizens

The Citizens Initiative Party

Initiative Party wants to avoid the jumbled state of confusion presently found in the political platforms of the two major parties.

The Political Platform of the Citizens Initiative Party

- **Term limits for all elected officials.**
- **= (Equal) taxation by percentage for all.**
- **Stand-alone legislation with sunset laws.**
- **Local "ownership" of government.**
- **Direct election of all public officials.**

The Citizens Initiative Party will keep its political platform basic, simple, easy to understand, and free of clutter.

XVIII. Other Considerations

Well-known organizations have mottoes or phrases that summarize the group's intentions. The Boy Scouts have "Be Prepared," and the Seabees have "Can Do." The Citizens Initiative Party will adopt the one word motto of the Northwest Company of the Canadian fur trade era —"**Perseverance**."

Like our new political party, the Northwest Company was an upstart operation that had to compete with much older, larger, and better-financed competitors. As is our desire in the political arena, the people of the Northwest Company were able to overcome their fur trading competitors because of innovative ideas and a novel approach to their market and the people they dealt with. Perseverance carried the day. Over time, the Northwest Company dominated the market and overcame its competition. In order to attain the success and accomplish the goals we envision, a great deal of perseverance will

The Citizens Initiative Party

be required by both the leadership and membership of the Citizens Initiative Party.

Political parties need a symbol, emblem or mascot for purposes of public recognition. The Citizens Initiative Party is no exception. The Democrats have their jackass. The Republicans have their elephant.

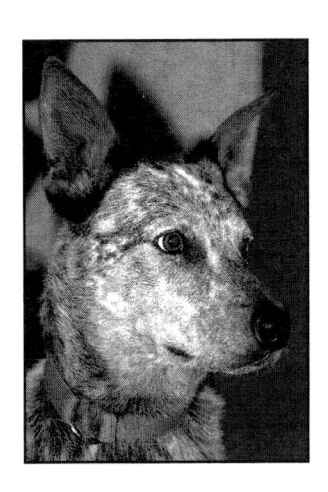

The Citizens Initiative Party will have as its mascot the Australian Cattle Dog, often referred to as the Australian Blue Heeler.

Why choose the Australian cattle dog for our mascot?

Within the chronology of dog breed development, the Australian Cattle Dog is a relatively new breed. With a bluish tint to its coat, this dog is a working dog. This breed was developed to work on cattle ranches, where it herds cattle by nipping at their heels — hence, Blue Heeler.

The Citizens Initiative Party is a new breed of political animal, and the Australian Blue Heeler has many of the characteristics we would like the public to associate with the Citizens Initiative Party. For instance, the Australian Blue Heeler is known for its tireless work ethic, its intelligence, courage, resilience, loyalty, toughness, and diligence.

Like our Citizens Initiative Party mascot, elected members of our party will herd the jackasses and the elephants, even though they are much larger beasts, by nipping at their heels relentlessly until we get them moving in the direction we envision. If, like our Blue Heeler mascot, we can keep on nipping at the heels of the two major parties, we can achieve the positive changes we seek and put an end to the presently fouled governmental systems.

Regardless of whether the Democrats have named their jackass or the Republicans have named their elephant, the Citizens Initiative Party's Australian Blue Heeler will be known as **Percy,** derived from our motto of "Perseverance."

Our theme song for rallies and get-togethers should be something both fun and rousing. My idea is to adapt the old theme song from the National Football League of the 1960s. The song is "Confidence" by the great composer Leon Carr. Just the title of this work sounds like the sort of thing that would fit in nicely with the image we wish to convey politically.

The Citizens Initiative Party membership pin will be a small equilateral triangle. This triangle will be symbolic of the fulcrum, part of the simple tool referred to

The Citizens Initiative Party

as the lever and fulcrum, a tool used to apply force to otherwise immovable objects. A fulcrum point can be moved to increase pressure on the object one is trying to move. The fulcrum point is also referred to as the *balance point*. One of the central ideas for forming the Citizens Initiative Party is to apply pressure on the two major parties while bringing balanced judgment and reality to the political process.

Because the Democrats have blue and the Republicans have red, the only primary color left for our use is yellow (we'll think in terms of golden) for the Citizens Initiative Party. The three vertices will indicate that this party, at long last, offers the third choice for voters. The top point will be either yellow or gold, the lower left point will be blue and the lower right will be red.

By finding the center of each of the sides of the triangle and connecting these points by lines, a diamond shape will be created in the center of the triangle along with two smaller triangles at each lower side. This diamond will be colored yellow or golden. Written inside will be the words "The Citizens Initiative Party." The left smaller triangle will be blue, and the right one will be red. **(See book cover.)**

Across the bottom of the triangle will be inscribed the party's motto: "Perseverance." Percy, our mascot, will be on the right side of the golden point.

Richard L. Freitag

This party pin will serve as a useful conversation starter when viewed on jackets and lapels.

The Citizens Initiative Party will issue plastic membership cards featuring Percy, our mascot; our motto "Perseverance;" and the triangular emblem of the party. In addition, these plastic credit-card-like cards will have the party member's name and membership number (assigned in chronological order as the members join).

I want card number one.

XIX. The Future and Your Choices

Ever since I can remember, there has been talk of creating a viable third party for the American political process. I am so frustrated by the lies, the rhetoric, and the wastefulness of the current government that I believe the time is *now* for the creation of this much-talked-about third party. Within these pages, I have offered my ideas for your consideration. My hope is that this is a place to begin discussion. Certainly some of my ideas are idealistic, perhaps even goofy or corny, and need to be revamped to be made workable. I'm okay with that. I can take criticism. All I'm offering here is a place to begin discussion and a place to begin what is needed at this time. But let us begin discussions and get this movement started! NOW!

Will those people who are not happy with our governmental systems simply continue to complain? Will those of us who are not happy continue to proclaim the self-fulfilling prophecy that there really is nothing we can do to change the way government systems are operated and perpetuated? Worse yet, will we just chuckle ruefully about the political quagmire and simply dismiss the mess as overwhelming? Will we allow the continued corruption, bribery, and slipshod governmental management practices to continue indefinitely?

Are we to blindly accept political favoritism, bribery, and influence peddling, thereby allowing these contemptible practices to continue in perpetuity unabated or, worse yet, to allow these disgusting governmental systems to become even more flagrant? Will we just cave in when members of the two major political parties claim we presently have the best government that is possible? And will we just give up when they assure us that they have our best interests in mind and that we as a fledgling political group can do no better? I certainly hope not!

The future of the Citizens Initiative Party, or any third party for that matter, belongs to those citizens who have had enough of the foulness of the governmental systems as they are operated today. Up until now, there have really been only *two* choices when entering the voting booth. Yes, there have been other parties besides the two major political parties. However, as previously argued and demonstrated, there are at this time only

The Citizens Initiative Party

two voting choices if realistic results from casting your vote truly matter to you.

Would a political party that gives voice to middle-class Americans who presently have no real voice in the politics of this nation affect a positive change on the American political landscape? Are sound reasoning, practicality, and results-oriented political analysis worthy goals in light of the radicalism that drives the present political and governmental systematized paralysis? Will the voting age American public respond favorably to a political party that takes the "high road" on the campaign trail? These questions are meaningless unless concerned citizens have the strength of will to make this new political option, the Citizens Initiative Party, available to the voting public.

Picture the following:

There are two railroad trains traveling down two sets of parallel tracks, one to the right and one to the left. The two sets of railroad tracks are very distant from one another, and the vast expanse between them seems to be widening. The area between the tracks remains uninhabited. The steel rails of the track system upon which both trains are traveling are very worn, almost to the point of being worn out. The rail beds consist of rotted or broken ties with loose spikes and plates that result in very dangerous conditions. While aware of the dangerous condition of these tracks, management of both railroads has made the decision to disregard the issue of danger. They believe these concerns are of secondary importance to the uninterrupted movement of the trains and the convenience of the passengers and the bags that are being carried.

A closer look reveals several interesting features concerning the trains and the tracks. Both locomotives are antiquated steam locomotives of the pre-Civil War era. These relics from the past lack the efficiency of the more current technology. Yet they continue on their course, slowly clanking and clunking along their dangerous pathway. No matter how much fuel they burn, these old engines are not capable of improving their efficiency or effectiveness. Increasing the quantity of fuel in the fire box only generates added heat and more soot, which flows out of the stack and pollutes the environment. Increasing the amount of fuel burned is a complete and total waste of resources. The clanking and clunking continue at the same old pace.

All passengers boarding the trains do so with the understanding that they are climbing aboard a train that is on a fixed and predetermined path. There can be no change in course because the rails only head in one direction. All of the passengers on both trains are soon covered with the soot and grime produced by the old steam engines. As more fuel is wastefully added, the contamination only gets worse, and the passengers on board only become dirtier.

Both antique locomotives are chugging along on a course they cannot change or alter. Locomotives, after all, cannot be steered, but must follow along their pre-set, predetermined pathways. Any change in course can occur only when a switchman throws a switch. But the old switchmen of the past are gone, and the switching mechanisms appear to be rusted and inoperable from disuse, so these old engines are destined to chug along on the same old one-directional, worn-out track system. Since there is no possibility of a change in course, the only certain thing for the future of these railroads is that the worn-out, dangerous track system will eventually break, causing a derailment. Will management blindly continue to avoid making the necessary repairs to the tracks until such a catastrophe occurs?

Probably.

An overview of the scene reveals yet other items of interest. To the left of the left-hand track and to the right of the right-hand track, a curious assortment of smaller vehicles is moving. These oddly diverse vehicles seem to be headed more or less in the same direction as the old steam locomotives. But many of these smaller vehicles appear to have lost their way or are operating in a state of confusion as they veer and swerve along their individual pathways. Some are as old as "high wheeler" bicycles, while others are as modern as scooters. Apart from traveling on either the far right or the far left of the two trains, their passengers have little in common with and very little chance of communicating with each other or with the passengers on the trains. Because these vehicles are so much smaller, they carry far fewer passengers than the trains.

Now envision entering into that ever-widening, uninhabited openness between the two old rail systems a state-of-the-art personal passenger jet aircraft. The aircraft is not shackled by the forces of gravity, but overcomes it. Nor is the jet aircraft on a predetermined path. This aircraft, though small in size, is extremely nimble and offers passengers an exhilarating ride. Passengers enter the aircraft clean and leave the aircraft just as clean.

Because it is not bound by old worn-out systems and predetermined paths, the agile aircraft can soar, dive, veer right or veer left as need be. The jet can distance itself from either or both of the old trains, should it so choose. If the passengers on board the plane see something of interest on one or the other of the old trains, the aircraft can get close to them, and the passengers aboard the aircraft can do this without getting covered in the soot and grime which is the train passengers' lot. The aircraft liberates its passengers from the entrapments of old, worn-out systems and the dilapidated, predetermined pathways. The passengers aboard the aircraft feel a sense of comfort and freedom in their surroundings. This is a truly fun and enjoyable ride for those who cannot feel a kinship with the passengers on the trains below.

You are the potential passenger. Which of these rides is of the most interest to you?

Get on board this new, modern, liberating vehicle with those who share your values, goals and ideals!

Can the Citizens Initiative Party become a reality? Should the Citizens Initiative Party become a reality? We know we should and that we can form this new political party, but the most important question of all undoubtedly is:

WILL WE?

It is time for mature adults to step into the fray between the fighting, immature children of the existing two major political parties.

If ever there was a need to create this third party and a perfect time to create this third party, that time is

NOW!

XX. Addendum

So that you can read and understand the laws and the basis for our democratic republic, The Constitution of the United States of America, along with all of the amendments to it, are printed on the following pages for your reading, your understanding, and your review.

All elected officials and military personnel swear by oath to uphold, defend, and protect this basic "law of the land." You will not find wording in this document that allows for its flexibility to fit with the current political climate of the day nor will you find language that allows for its interpretation based on political correctness or otherwise. It is written in plain enough language that it can readily be understood by the citizens of this nation for whom it was written. This is the Constitution of your country. Read it. Understand it. Know it. Cherish it.

Although there are those who find this document to be an interference in their political agenda and believe it should be subjected to interpretation based upon *their current political agenda*, it has nevertheless withstood

The Citizens Initiative Party

the test of time. All American citizens should know and understand what it says for their own good.

Much of the Constitution of the United States of America is based on the Declaration of Independence. It too is printed on the following pages for you to read and understand.

Constitution of the United States of America

<u>Underlined</u> text has been superseded by amendments

Preamble

We the people of the United States, in order to form a more perfect union, establish justice, insure domestic tranquility, provide for the common defense, promote the general welfare, and secure the blessings of liberty to ourselves and our posterity, do ordain and establish this Constitution for the United States of America.

Article I

Section 1

All legislative powers herein granted shall be vested in a Congress of the United States, which shall consist of a Senate and House of Representatives.

Section 2

The House of Representatives shall be composed of members chosen every second year by the people of the several states, and the electors in each state shall have the qualifications requisite for electors of the most numerous branch of the state legislature.

No person shall be a Representative who shall not have attained to the age of twenty-five years, and been seven years a citizen of the United States, and who shall not, when elected, be an inhabitant of that state in which he shall be chosen.

<u>Representatives and direct taxes shall be apportioned among the several states which may be included within this union, according to their respective numbers, which shall be determined by adding to the whole number of free persons, including those bound to service for a term of years, and excluding Indians not taxed, three-fifths of all other persons.</u> The actual enumeration shall be made within three years after the first meeting of the Congress of the United States, and within every subsequent term of ten years, in such manner as they shall by law direct. The number of Representatives shall not exceed one for every thirty thousand, but each state shall have at least one Representative; and until such enumeration shall be made, the state of New Hampshire shall be entitled to choose three, Massachusetts eight, Rhode Island and Providence Plantations one, Connecticut five, New York six, New Jersey four, Pennsylvania eight, Delaware one,

Maryland six, Virginia ten, North Carolina five, South Carolina five, and Georgia three.

When vacancies happen in the representation from any state, the executive authority thereof shall issue writs of election to fill such vacancies.

The House of Representatives shall choose their speaker and other officers; and shall have the sole power of impeachment.

Section 3

The Senate of the United States shall be composed of two Senators from each state, <u>chosen by the legislature thereof</u> for six years; and each Senator shall have one vote.

Immediately after they shall be assembled in consequence of the first election, they shall be divided as equally as may be into three classes. The seats of the Senators of the first class shall be vacated at the expiration of the second year, of the second class at the expiration of the fourth year, and of the third class at the expiration of the sixth year, so that one-third may be chosen every second year; <u>and if vacancies happen by resignation, or otherwise, during the recess of the legislature of any state, the executive thereof may make temporary appointments until the next meeting of the legislature,</u>

<u>which shall then fill such vacancies</u>.

No person shall be a Senator who shall not have attained to the age of thirty years, and been nine years a citizen of the United States, and who shall not, when elected, be an inhabitant of that state for which he shall be chosen.

The Vice President of the United States shall be President of the Senate, but shall have no vote, unless they are equally divided.

The Senate shall choose their other officers, and also a President pro tempore, in the absence of the Vice President, or when he shall exercise the office of President of the United States.

The Senate shall have the sole power to try all impeachments. When sitting for that purpose, they shall be on oath or affirmation. When the President of the United States is tried, the Chief Justice shall preside; and no person shall be convicted without the concurrence of two-thirds of the members present.

Judgment in cases of impeachment shall not extend further than to removal from office, and disqualification to hold and enjoy any office of honor, trust or profit under the United States; but the party convicted shall nevertheless be liable and subject to indictment, trial, judgment and punishment, according to law.

Section 4

The times, places and manner of holding elections for Senators and Representatives shall be prescribed in each state by the legislature thereof; but the Congress may at any time by law make or alter such regulations, except as to the places of choosing Senators.

The Congress shall assemble at least once in every year, and such meeting shall <u>be on the first Monday in December,</u> unless they shall by law appoint a different day.

Section 5

Each House shall be the judge of the elections, returns and qualifications of its own members, and a majority of each shall constitute a quorum to do business; but a smaller number may adjourn from day to day, and may be authorized to compel the attendance of absent members, in such manner, and under such penalties as each House may provide.

Each House may determine the rules of its proceedings, punish its members for disorderly behavior, and, with the concurrence of two-thirds, expel a member.

Each House shall keep a journal of its proceedings, and from time to time publish the same, excepting such parts as may in their judgment require secrecy; and the yeas and nays of the members of either House on any question shall, at the desire of one-fifth of those present, be entered on the journal.

Neither House, during the session of Congress, shall, without the consent of the other, adjourn for more than three days, nor to any other place than that in which the two Houses shall be sitting.

Section 6

The Senators and Representatives shall receive a compensation for their services, to be ascertained by law, and paid out of the treasury of the United States. They shall in all cases, except treason, felony and breach of the peace, be privileged from arrest during their attendance at the session of their respective Houses, and in going to and returning from the same; and for any speech or debate in either House, they shall not be questioned in any other place.

No Senator or Representative shall, during the time for which he was elected, be appointed to any civil office under the authority of the United States, which shall have been created, or the emoluments whereof shall have been increased during such time; and no person holding any office under the United States, shall be a member of either House during his continuance in office.

Section 7

All bills for raising revenue shall originate in the House of Representatives; but the Senate may propose or concur with amendments as on other bills.

Every bill which shall have passed the House of Representatives and the Senate, shall, before it become a law, be presented to the President of the United States: If he approve he shall sign it, but if not he shall return it, with his objections to that House in which it shall have originated, who shall enter the objections at large on their journal, and proceed to reconsider it. If after such reconsideration two-thirds of that House shall agree to pass the bill, it shall be sent, together with the objections, to the other House, by which it shall likewise be reconsidered, and if approved by two-thirds of that House, it shall become a law. But in all such cases the votes of both Houses shall be determined by yeas and nays, and the names of the persons voting for and against the bill shall be entered on the journal of each House respectively. If any bill shall not be returned by the President within ten days (Sundays excepted) after it shall have been presented to him, the same shall be a law, in like manner as if he had signed it, unless the Congress by their adjournment prevent its return, in which case it shall not be a law.

Every order, resolution, or vote to which the concurrence of the Senate and House of Representatives may be necessary (except on a question of adjournment) shall be presented to the President of the United States; and before the same shall take effect, shall be approved by him, or being disapproved by him, shall be reposed by two-thirds of the Senate and House of Representatives, according to the rules and limitations prescribed in the case of a bill.

Section 8

The Congress shall have power to lay and collect taxes, duties, imposts and excises, to pay the debts and provide for the common defense and general welfare of the United States; but all duties, imposts and excises shall be uniform throughout the United States;

To borrow money on the credit of the United States;

To regulate commerce with foreign nations, and among the several states, and with the Indian tribes;

To establish an uniform rule of naturalization, and uniform laws on the subject of bankruptcies throughout the United States;

To coin money, regulate the value thereof, and of foreign coin, and fix the standard of weights and measures;

To provide for the punishment of counterfeiting the securities and current coin of the United States;

To establish post offices and post roads;

To promote the progress of science and useful arts, by securing for limited times to authors and inventors the exclusive right to their respective writings and discoveries;

To constitute tribunals inferior to the Supreme Court;

To define and punish piracies and felonies committed on the high seas, and offences against the law of nations;

To declare war, grant letters of marque and reprisal, and make rules concerning captures on land and water;

To raise and support armies, but no appropriation of money to that use shall be for a longer term than two years;

To provide and maintain a navy;

To make rules for the government and regulation of the land and naval forces;

To provide for calling forth the militia to execute the laws of the union, suppress insurrections and repel invasions;

To provide for organizing, arming, and disciplining, the militia, and for governing such part of them as may be employed in the service of the United States, reserving to the states respectively, the appointment of the officers, and the authority of training the militia according to the discipline prescribed by Congress;

To exercise exclusive legislation in all cases whatsoever, over such district (not exceeding ten miles square) as may, by cession of particular states, and the acceptance of Congress, become the seat of the government of the United States, and to exercise like authority over all places purchased by the consent of the legislature of the state in which the same shall be, for the erection of forts, magazines, arsenals, dockyards, and other needful buildings; — And

To make all laws which shall be necessary and proper for carrying into execution the foregoing powers, and all other powers vested by this Constitution in the government of the United States, or in any department or officer thereof.

Section 9

The migration or importation of such persons as any of the states now existing shall think proper to admit, shall not be prohibited by the Congress prior to the year one thousand eight hundred and eight, but a tax or duty may be imposed on such importation, not exceeding ten dollars for each person.

The privilege of the writ of habeas corpus shall not be suspended, unless when in cases of rebellion or invasion the public safety may require it.

No bill of attainder or ex post facto law shall be passed.

No capitation, or other direct, tax shall be laid, <u>unless in proportion to the census or enumeration herein before directed to be taken.</u>

No tax or duty shall be laid on articles exported from any state.

No preference shall be given by any regulation of commerce or revenue to the ports of one state over those of another; nor shall vessels bound to, or from, one state, be obliged to enter, clear, or pay duties in another.

No money shall be drawn from the treasury, but in consequence of appropriations made by law; and a regular statement and account of the receipts and expenditures of all public money shall be published from time to time.

No title of nobility shall be granted by the United States; and no person holding any office of profit or trust under them, shall, without the consent of the Congress, accept of any present, emolument, office, or title, of any kind whatever, from any king, prince, or foreign state.

Section 10

No state shall enter into any treaty, alliance, or confederation; grant letters of marque and reprisal; coin money; emit bills of credit; make anything but gold and silver coin a tender in payment of debts; pass any bill of attainder, ex post facto law, or law impairing the obligation of contracts, or grant any title of nobility.

No state shall, without the consent of the Congress, lay any imposts or duties on imports or exports, except what may be absolutely necessary for executing its inspection laws; and the net produce of all duties and imposts, laid by any state on imports or exports, shall be for the use of the treasury of the United States; and all such laws shall be subject to the revision and control of the Congress.

No state shall, without the consent of Congress, lay any duty of tonnage, keep troops, or ships of war in time of peace, enter into any agreement or compact with another state, or with a foreign power, or engage in war, unless actually invaded, or in such imminent danger as will not admit of delay.

Article II

Section 1

The executive power shall be vested in a President of the United States of America. He shall hold his office during the term of four years, and, together with the Vice President, chosen for the same term, be elected, as follows:

Each state shall appoint, in such manner as the legislature thereof may direct, a number of electors, equal to the whole number of Senators and Representatives to which the state may be entitled in the Congress; but no Senator or Representative, or person holding an office of trust or profit under the United States, shall be appointed an elector.

<u>The electors shall meet in their respective states, and vote by ballot for two persons, of whom one at least shall not be an inhabitant of the same state with themselves. And they shall make a list of all the persons voted for, and of the number of votes for each; which list they shall sign and certify, and transmit sealed to the seat of the government of the United States, directed to the President of the Senate. The President of the Senate shall, in the presence of the Senate and House of Representatives, open all the certificates, and the votes shall then be counted. The person having the greatest number of votes shall be the President, if such number be a majority of the whole number of electors appointed; and if there be more than one who have such majority, and have an equal number of votes, then the House of Representatives shall immediately choose by ballot one of them for President; and if no person have a majority, then from the five highest on the list the said House shall in like manner choose the President. But in choosing the President, the votes shall be taken by states, the</u>

representation from each state having one vote. A quorum for this purpose shall consist of a member or members from two-thirds of the states, and a majority of all the states shall be necessary to a choice. In every case, after the choice of the President, the person having the greatest number of votes of the electors shall be the Vice President. But if there should remain two or more who have equal votes, the Senate shall choose from them by ballot the Vice President.

The Congress may determine the time of choosing the electors, and the day on which they shall give their votes; which day shall be the same throughout the United States.

No person except a natural born citizen, or a citizen of the United States, at the time of the adoption of this Constitution, shall be eligible to the office of President; neither shall any person be eligible to that office who shall not have attained to the age of thirty-five years, and been fourteen years a resident within the United States.

In case of the removal of the President from office, or of his death, resignation, or inability to discharge the powers and duties of the said office, the same shall devolve on the Vice President, and the Congress may by law provide for the case of removal, death, resignation or inability, both of the President and Vice President, declaring what officer shall then act as President, and such officer shall act accordingly, until the disability be removed, or a President shall be elected.

The President shall, at stated times, receive for his services, a compensation, which shall neither be increased nor diminished during the period for which he shall have been elected, and he shall not receive within that period any other emolument from the United States, or any of them.

Before he enter on the execution of his office, he shall take the following oath or affirmation: — "I do solemnly swear (or affirm) that I will faithfully execute the office of President of the United States, and will to the best of my ability, preserve, protect and defend the Constitution of the United States."

Section 2

The President shall be commander in chief of the Army and Navy of the United States, and of the militia of the several states, when called into the actual service of the United States; he may require the opinion, in writing, of the principal officer in each of the executive departments, upon any subject relating to the duties of their respective offices, and he shall have power to grant reprieves and pardons for offences against the United States, except in cases of impeachment.

He shall have power, by and with the advice and

consent of the Senate, to make treaties, provided two-thirds of the Senators present concur; and he shall nominate, and by and with the advice and consent of the Senate, shall appoint ambassadors, other public ministers and consuls, judges of the Supreme Court, and all other officers of the United States, whose appointments are not herein otherwise provided for, and which shall be established by law; but the Congress may by law vest the appointment of such inferior officers, as they think proper, in the President alone, in the courts of law, or in the heads of departments.

The President shall have power to fill up all vacancies that may happen during the recess of the Senate, by granting commissions which shall expire at the end of their next session.

Section 3

He shall from time to time give to the Congress information of the state of the union, and recommend to their consideration such measures as he shall judge necessary and expedient; he may, on extraordinary occasions, convene both Houses, or either of them, and in case of disagreement between them, with respect to the time of adjournment, he may adjourn them to such time as he shall think proper; he shall receive ambassadors and other public ministers; he shall take care that the laws be faithfully executed, and shall commission all the officers of the United States.

Section 4
The President, Vice President and all civil officers of the United States, shall be removed from office on impeachment for, and conviction of, treason, bribery, or other high crimes and misdemeanors.

Article III

Section 1
The judicial power of the United States shall be vested in one Supreme Court, and in such inferior courts as the Congress may from time to time ordain and establish. The judges, both of the supreme and inferior courts, shall hold their offices during good behavior, and shall, at stated times, receive for their services a compensation, which shall not be diminished during their continuance in office.

Section 2
The judicial power shall extend to all cases, in law and equity, arising under this Constitution, the laws of the United States, and treaties made, or which shall be made, under their authority; — to all cases affecting ambassadors, other public ministers and consuls; — to all cases of admiralty and maritime jurisdiction; — to controversies

to which the United States shall be a party; — to controversies between two or more states; — <u>between a state and citizens of another state</u>; — between citizens of different states; — between citizens of the same state claiming lands under grants of different states, and between a state, or the citizens thereof, and foreign states, citizens or subjects.

In all cases affecting ambassadors, other public ministers and consuls, and those in which a state shall be party, the Supreme Court shall have original jurisdiction. In all the other cases before mentioned, the Supreme Court shall have appellate jurisdiction, both as to law and fact, with such exceptions, and under such regulations as the congress shall make.

The trial of all crimes, except in cases of impeachment, shall be by jury; and such trial shall be held in the state where the said crimes shall have been committed; but when not committed within any state, the trial shall be at such place or places as the congress may by law have directed.

Section 3

Treason against the United States shall consist only in levying war against them, or in adhering to their enemies, giving them aid and comfort. No person shall be convicted of treason unless on the testimony of two witnesses to the same overt act, or on confession in open court.

The Congress shall have power to declare the punishment of treason, but no attainder of treason shall work corruption of blood, or forfeiture except during the life of the person attainted.

Article IV

Section 1

Full faith and credit shall be given in each state to the public acts, records, and judicial proceedings of every other state. And the Congress may by general laws prescribe the manner in which such acts, records and proceedings shall be proved, and the effect thereof.

Section 2

The citizens of each state shall be entitled to all privileges and immunities of citizens in the several states.

A person charged in any state with treason, felony, or other crime, who shall flee from justice, and be found in another state, shall on demand of the executive authority of the state from which he fled, be delivered up, to be removed to the state having jurisdiction of the crime.

<u>No person held to service or labor in one state, under the laws thereof, escaping into another, shall, in</u>

<u>consequence of any law or regulation therein, be discharged from such service or labor, but shall be delivered up on claim of the party to whom such service or labor may be due</u>.

Section 3

New states may be admitted by the Congress into this union; but no new state shall be formed or erected within the jurisdiction of any other state; nor any state be formed by the junction of two or more states, or parts of states, without the consent of the legislatures of the states concerned as well as of the Congress.

The Congress shall have power to dispose of and make all needful rules and regulations respecting the territory or other property belonging to the United States; and nothing in this Constitution shall be so construed as to prejudice any claims of the United States, or of any particular state.

Section 4

The United States shall guarantee to every state in this union a republican form of government, and shall protect each of them against invasion; and on application of the legislature, or of the executive (when the legislature cannot be convened), against domestic violence.

Article V

The Congress, whenever two-thirds of both houses shall deem it necessary, shall propose amendments to this Constitution, or, on the application of the legislatures of two-thirds of the several states, shall call a convention for proposing amendments, which, in either case, shall be valid to all intents and purposes, as part of this Constitution, when ratified by the legislatures of three-fourths of the several states, or by conventions in three-fourths thereof, as the one or the other mode of ratification may be proposed by the Congress; provided that no amendment which may be made prior to the year one thousand eight hundred and eight shall in any manner affect the first and fourth clauses in the ninth Section of the first Article; and that no state, without its consent, shall be deprived of its equal suffrage in the Senate.

Article VI

All debts contracted and engagements entered into, before the adoption of this Constitution, shall be as valid against the United States under this Constitution, as under the Confederation.

This Constitution, and the laws of the United States which shall be made in pursuance thereof; and all treaties made, or which shall be made, under the authority of the United States, shall be the supreme law of the land; and the judges in every state shall be bound thereby, anything in the Constitution or laws of any State to the contrary notwithstanding.

The Senators and Representatives before mentioned, and the members of the several state legislatures, and all executive and judicial officers, both of the United States and of the several states, shall be bound by oath or affirmation, to support this Constitution; but no religious test shall ever be required as a qualification to any office or public trust under the United States.

Article VII

The ratification of the conventions of nine states shall be sufficient for the establishment of this Constitution between the states so ratifying the same.

Constitutional Amendments

Bill of Rights (Amendments I-X)

Amendment I

Congress shall make no law respecting an establishment of religion, or prohibiting the free exercise thereof; or abridging the freedom of speech, or of the press; or the right of the people peaceably to assemble, and to petition the government for a redress of grievances.

Amendment II

A well-regulated militia, being necessary to the security of a free state, the right of the people to keep and bear arms, shall not be infringed.

Amendment III

No soldier shall, in time of peace be quartered in any house, without the consent of the owner, nor in time of war, but in a manner to be prescribed by law.

Amendment IV

The right of the people to be secure in their persons, houses, papers, and effects, against unreasonable searches and seizures, shall not be violated, and no warrants shall issue, but upon probable cause, supported by oath or affirmation, and particularly describing the place to be searched, and the persons or things to be seized.

Amendment V

No person shall be held to answer for a capital, or otherwise infamous crime, unless on a presentment or indictment of a grand jury, except in cases arising in the land or naval forces, or in the militia, when in actual service in time of war or public danger; nor shall any person be subject for the same offense to be twice put in jeopardy of life or limb; nor shall be compelled in any criminal case to be a witness against himself, nor be deprived of life, liberty, or property, without due process of law; nor shall private property be taken for public use, without just compensation.

Amendment VI

In all criminal prosecutions, the accused shall enjoy the right to a speedy and public trial, by an impartial jury of the state and district wherein the crime shall have been committed, which district shall have been previously ascertained by law, and to be informed of the nature and cause of the accusation; to be confronted with the witnesses against him; to have compulsory process for obtaining witnesses in his favor, and to have the assistance of counsel for his defense.

Amendment VII

In suits at common law, where the value in controversy shall exceed twenty dollars, the right of trial by jury shall be preserved, and no fact tried by a jury, shall be otherwise reexamined in any court of the United States, than according to the rules of the common law.

Amendment VIII

Excessive bail shall not be required, nor excessive fines imposed, nor cruel and unusual punishments inflicted.

Amendment IX

The enumeration in the Constitution, of certain rights, shall not be construed to deny or disparage others retained by the people.

Amendment X

The powers not delegated to the United States by the Constitution, nor prohibited by it to the states, are reserved to the states respectively, or to the people.

Amendment XI
(1798)

The judicial power of the United States shall not be construed to extend to any suit in law or equity, commenced or prosecuted against one of the United States by citizens of another state, or by citizens or subjects of any foreign state.

Amendment XII
(1804)

The electors shall meet in their respective states and vote by ballot for President and Vice President, one of whom, at least, shall not be an inhabitant of the same state with themselves; they shall name in their ballots the person voted for as President, and in distinct ballots the person voted for as Vice President, and they shall make distinct lists of all persons voted for as President, and of all persons voted for as Vice President, and of the number of votes for each, which lists they shall sign and certify, and transmit sealed to the seat of the government of the United States, directed to the President of the Senate;—The President of the Senate shall, in the presence of the Senate and House of Representatives, open all the certificates and the votes shall then be counted;—the person having the greatest number of votes for President, shall be the President, if such number be a majority of the whole number of electors appointed; and if no person have such majority, then from the persons having the highest numbers not exceeding three on the list of those voted for as President, the House of Representatives shall choose immediately, by ballot, the President. But in choosing the President, the votes shall be taken by states, the representation from each state having one vote; a quorum for this purpose shall consist of a member or members from two-thirds of the states, and a majority of all the states shall be necessary to a choice. And if the House of Representatives shall not choose a President whenever the right of choice shall devolve upon them, before the fourth day of March next following, then the Vice President shall act as President, as in the case of the death or other constitutional disability of the President. The person having the greatest number of votes as Vice President shall be the Vice President, if such number be a majority of the whole number of electors appointed, and if no person have a majority, then from the two highest numbers on the list, the Senate shall choose the Vice President; a quorum for the purpose shall consist of two-thirds of the whole number of Senators, and a majority of the whole number shall be necessary to a choice. But no person constitutionally ineligible to the office of President shall be eligible to that of Vice President of the United States.

Amendment XIII
(1865)

Section 1. Neither slavery nor involuntary servitude, except as a punishment for crime whereof the party shall have been duly convicted, shall exist within the United States, or any place subject to their jurisdiction.

Section 2. Congress shall have power to enforce this article by appropriate legislation.

Amendment XIV
(1868)

Section 1. All persons born or naturalized in the United States, and subject to the jurisdiction thereof, are citizens of the United States and of the state wherein they reside. No state shall make or enforce any law which shall abridge the privileges or immunities of citizens of the United States; nor shall any state deprive any person of life, liberty, or property, without due process of law; nor deny to any person within its jurisdiction the equal protection of the laws.

Section 2. Representatives shall be apportioned among the several states according to their respective numbers, counting the whole number of persons in each state, excluding Indians not taxed. But when the right to vote at any election for the choice of electors for President and Vice President of the United States, Representatives in Congress, the executive and judicial officers of a state, or the members of the legislature thereof, is denied to any of the male inhabitants of such state, being twenty-one years of age, and citizens of the United States, or in any way abridged, except for participation in rebellion, or other crime, the basis of representation therein shall be reduced in the proportion which the number of such male citizens shall bear to the whole number of male citizens twenty-one years of age in such state.

Section 3. No person shall be a Senator or Representative in Congress, or elector of President and Vice President, or hold any office, civil or military, under the United States, or under any state, who, having previously taken an oath, as a member of Congress, or as an officer of the United States, or as a member of any state legislature, or as an executive or judicial officer of any state, to support the Constitution of the United States, shall have engaged in insurrection or rebellion against the same, or given aid or comfort to the enemies thereof. But Congress may by a vote of two-thirds of each House, remove such disability.

Section 4. The validity of the public debt of the United States, authorized by law, including debts incurred for payment of pensions and bounties for services in suppressing insurrection or rebellion, shall not be questioned. But neither the United States nor any state shall assume or pay any debt or obligation incurred in aid of insurrection or rebellion against the United States, or any claim for the loss or emancipation of any slave; but all such debts, obligations and claims shall be held illegal and void.

Section 5. The Congress shall have power to enforce, by appropriate legislation, the provisions of this article.

Amendment XV
(1870)

Section 1. The right of citizens of the United States to vote shall not be denied or abridged by the United States or by any state on account of race, color, or previous condition of servitude.

Section 2. The Congress shall have power to enforce this article by appropriate legislation.

Amendment XVI
(1913)

The Congress shall have power to lay and collect taxes on incomes, from whatever source derived, without apportionment among the several states, and without regard to any census of enumeration.

Amendment XVII
(1913)

The Senate of the United States shall be composed of two Senators from each state, elected by the people thereof, for six years; and each Senator shall have one vote. The electors in each state shall have the qualifications requisite for electors of the most numerous branch of the state legislatures.

When vacancies happen in the representation of any state in the Senate, the executive authority of such state shall issue writs of election to fill such vacancies: Provided, that the legislature of any state may empower the executive thereof to make temporary appointments until the people fill the vacancies by election as the legislature may direct.

This amendment shall not be so construed as to affect the election or term of any Senator chosen before it becomes valid as part of the Constitution.

Amendment XVIII
(1919)

Section 1. After one year from the ratification of this article the manufacture, sale, or transportation of intoxicating liquors within, the importation thereof into, or the exportation thereof from the United States and all territory subject to the jurisdiction thereof for beverage purposes is hereby prohibited.

Section 2. The Congress and the several states shall have concurrent power to enforce this article by appropriate legislation.

Section 3. This article shall be inoperative unless it shall have been ratified as an amendment to the Constitution by the legislatures of the several states, as provided in the Constitution, within seven years from the date of the submission hereof to the states by the Congress.

Amendment XIX
(1920)

The right of citizens of the United States to vote shall not be denied or abridged by the United States or by any state on account of sex.

Congress shall have power to enforce this article by appropriate legislation.

Amendment XX
(1933)

Section 1. The terms of the President and Vice President shall end at noon on the 20th day of January, and the terms of Senators and Representatives at noon on the 3rd day of January, of the years in which such terms would have ended if this article had not been ratified; and the terms of their successors shall then begin.

Section 2. The Congress shall assemble at least once in every year, and such meeting shall begin at noon on the 3rd day of January, unless they shall by law appoint a different day.

Section 3. If, at the time fixed for the beginning of the term of the President, the President-elect shall have died, the Vice President-elect shall become President. If a President shall not have been chosen before the time fixed for the beginning of his term, or if the President-elect shall have failed to qualify, then the Vice President-elect shall act as President until a President shall have qualified; and the Congress may by law provide for the case wherein neither a President-elect nor a Vice President-elect shall have qualified, declaring who shall then act as President, or the manner in which one who is to act shall be selected, and such person shall act accordingly until a President or Vice President shall have qualified.

Section 4. The Congress may by law provide for the case of the death of any of the persons from whom the House of Representatives may choose a President whenever the right of choice shall have devolved upon them, and for the case of the death of any of the persons from whom the Senate may choose a Vice President whenever the right of choice shall have devolved upon them.

Section 5. Sections 1 and 2 shall take effect on the 15th day of October following the ratification of this article.

Section 6. This article shall be inoperative unless it shall have been ratified as an amendment to the Constitution by the legislatures of three-fourths of the several states within seven years from the date of its submission.

Amendment XXI
(1933)

Section 1. The eighteenth article of amendment to the Constitution of the United States is hereby repealed.

Section 2. The transportation or importation into any state, territory, or possession of the United States for delivery or use therein of intoxicating liquors, in violation of the laws thereof, is hereby prohibited.

Section 3. This article shall be inoperative unless it shall have been ratified as an amendment to the Constitution by conventions in the several states, as provided in the Constitution, within seven years from the date of the submission hereof to the states by the Congress.

Amendment XXII
(1951)

Section 1. No person shall be elected to the office of the President more than twice, and no person who has held the office of President, or acted as President, for more than two years of a term to which some other person was elected President shall be elected to the office of the President more than once. But this article shall not apply to any person holding the office of President when this article was proposed by the Congress, and shall not prevent any person who may be holding the office of President, or acting as President, during the term within which this article becomes operative from holding the office of President or acting as President during the remainder of such term.

Section 2. This article shall be inoperative unless it shall have been ratified as an amendment to the Constitution by the legislatures of three-fourths of the several states within seven years from the date of its submission to the states by the Congress.

Amendment XXIII
(1961)

Section 1. The District constituting the seat of government of the United States shall appoint in such manner as the Congress may direct:

A number of electors of President and Vice President equal to the whole number of Senators and Representatives in Congress to which the District would be entitled if it were a state, but in no event more than the least populous state; they shall be in addition to those appointed by the states, but they shall be considered, for the purposes of the election of President and Vice President, to be electors appointed by a state; and they shall meet in the District and perform such duties as provided by the twelfth article of amendment.

Section 2. The Congress shall have power to enforce this article by appropriate legislation.

Amendment XXIV
(1964)

Section 1. The right of citizens of the United States to vote in any primary or other election for President or Vice President, for electors for President or Vice President, or for Senator or Representative in Congress, shall not be denied or abridged by the United States or any state by reason of failure to pay any poll tax or other tax.

Section 2. The Congress shall have power to enforce this article by appropriate legislation.

Richard L. Freitag

Amendment XXV
(1967)

Section 1. In case of the removal of the President from office or of his death or resignation, the Vice President shall become President.

Section 2. Whenever there is a vacancy in the office of the Vice President, the President shall nominate a Vice President who shall take office upon confirmation by a majority vote of both Houses of Congress.

Section 3. Whenever the President transmits to the President pro tempore of the Senate and the Speaker of the House of Representatives his written declaration that he is unable to discharge the powers and duties of his office, and until he transmits to them a written declaration to the contrary, such powers and duties shall be discharged by the Vice President as Acting President.

Section 4. Whenever the Vice President and a majority of either the principal officers of the executive departments or of such other body as Congress may by law provide, transmit to the President pro tempore of the Senate and the Speaker of the House of Representatives their written declaration that the President is unable to discharge the powers and duties of his office, the Vice President shall immediately assume the powers and duties of the office as Acting President.

Thereafter, when the President transmits to the President pro tempore of the Senate and the Speaker of the House of Representatives his written declaration that no inability exists, he shall resume the powers and duties of his office unless the Vice President and a majority of either the principal officers of the executive department or of such other body as Congress may by law provide, transmit within four days to the President pro tempore of the Senate and the Speaker of the House of Representatives their written declaration that the President is unable to discharge the powers and duties of his office. Thereupon Congress shall decide the issue, assembling within forty-eight hours for that purpose if not in session. If the Congress, within twenty-one days after receipt of the latter written declaration, or, if Congress is not in session, within twenty-one days after Congress is required to assemble, determines by two-thirds vote of both Houses that the President is unable to discharge the powers and duties of his office, the Vice President shall continue to discharge the same as Acting President; otherwise, the President shall resume the powers and duties of his office.

Amendment XXVI
(1971)

Section 1. The right of citizens of the United States, who are 18 years of age or older, to vote, shall not be denied or abridged by the United States or any state on account of age.

Section 2. The Congress shall have the power to enforce this article by appropriate legislation.

Amendment XXVII
(1992)

No law varying the compensation for the services of the Senators and Representatives shall take effect until an election of Representatives shall have intervened.

Declaration of Independence

Adopted in Congress July 4, 1776

The Unanimous Declaration of the Thirteen United States of America

When, in the course of human events, it becomes necessary for one people to dissolve the political bands which have connected them with another, and to assume among the powers of the earth, the separate and equal station to which the laws of nature and of nature's God entitle them, a decent respect to the opinions of mankind requires that they should declare the causes which impel them to the separation.

We hold these truths to be self-evident, that all men are created equal, that they are endowed by their Creator with certain unalienable rights, that among these are life, liberty and the pursuit of happiness. That to secure these rights, government is instituted among men, deriving their just powers from the consent of the governed. That whenever any form of government becomes destructive to these ends, it is the right of the people to alter or to abolish it, and to institute new government, laying its foundation on such principles and organizing its powers in such form, as to them shall seem most likely to affect their safety and happiness. Prudence, indeed, will dictate that governments long established should not be changed for light and transient causes; and accordingly all experience hath shown that mankind are more disposed to suffer, while evils are sufferable, than to right themselves by abolishing the forms to which they are accustomed. But when a long train of abuses and usurpations, pursuing invariably the same object evinces a design to reduce them under absolute despotism, it is their right, it is their duty, to throw off such government, and to provide new guards for their future security. — Such has been the patient sufferance of these colonies; and such is now the necessity which constrains them to alter their former systems of government. The history of the present King of Great Britain is a history of repeated injuries and usurpations, all having in direct object the establishment of an absolute tyranny over these states. To prove this, let facts be submitted to a candid world.

He has refused his assent to laws, the most wholesome and necessary for the public good.

He has forbidden his governors to pass laws of immediate and pressing importance, unless suspended in their operation till his assent should be obtained; and when so suspended, he has utterly neglected to attend to them.

He has refused to pass other laws for the accommodation of large districts of people, unless those people would relinquish the right of representation in the legislature, a right inestimable to them and formidable to tyrants only.

He has called together legislative bodies at places unusual, uncomfortable, and distant from the depository of their public records, for the sole purpose of fatiguing them into compliance with his measures.

He has dissolved representative houses repeatedly, for opposing with manly firmness his invasions on the rights of the people.

He has refused for a long time, after such dissolutions, to cause others to be elected; whereby the legislative powers, incapable of annihilation, have returned to the people at large for their exercise; the state remaining in the meantime exposed to all the dangers of invasion from without, and convulsions within.

He has endeavored to prevent the population of these states; for that purpose obstructing the laws for naturalization of foreigners; refusing to pass others to encourage their migration hither, and raising the conditions of new appropriations of lands.

He has obstructed the administration of justice, by

refusing his assent to laws for establishing judiciary powers.

He has made judges dependent on his will alone, for the tenure of their offices, and the amount and payment of their salaries.

He has erected a multitude of new offices, and sent hither swarms of officers to harass our people, and eat out their substance.

He has kept among us, in times of peace, standing armies without the consent of our legislature.

He has affected to render the military independent of and superior to civil power.

He has combined with others to subject us to a jurisdiction foreign to our constitution, and unacknowledged by our laws; giving his assent to their acts of pretended legislation:

For quartering large bodies of armed troops among us:

For protecting them, by mock trial, from punishment for any murders which they should commit on the inhabitants of these states:

For cutting off our trade with all parts of the world:

For imposing taxes on us without our consent:

For depriving us in many cases, of the benefits of trial by jury:

For transporting us beyond seas to be tried for

pretended offenses:

For abolishing the free system of English laws in a neighboring province, establishing therein an arbitrary government, and enlarging its boundaries so as to render it at once an example and fit instrument for introducing the same absolute rule in these colonies:

For taking away our charters, abolishing our most valuable laws, and altering fundamentally the forms of our governments:

For suspending our own legislatures and declaring themselves invested with power to legislate for us in all cases whatsoever.

He has abdicated government here, by declaring us out of his protection and waging war against us.

He has plundered our seas, ravaged our coasts, burned our towns, and destroyed the lives of our people.

He is at this time transporting large armies of foreign mercenaries to complete the works of death, desolation and tyranny, already begun with circumstances of cruelty and perfidy scarcely paralleled in the most barbarous ages, and totally unworthy of the head of a civilized nation.

He has constrained our fellow citizens taken captive on the high seas to bear arms against their country, to become the executioners of their friends and brethren, or to fall themselves by their hands.

Richard L. Freitag

He has excited domestic insurrections amongst us, and has endeavored to bring on the inhabitants of our frontiers, the merciless Indian savages, whose known rule of warfare, is undistinguished destruction of all ages, sexes and conditions.

In every stage of these oppressions we have petitioned for redress in the most humble terms: our repeated petitions have been answered only by repeated injury. A prince, whose character is thus marked by every act which may define a tyrant, is unfit to be the ruler of a free people.

Nor have we been wanting in attention to our British brethren. We have warned them from time to time of attempts by their legislature to extend an unwarrantable jurisdiction over us. We have reminded them of the circumstances of our emigration and settlement here. We have appealed to their native justice and magnanimity, and we have conjured them by the ties of our common kindred to disavow these usurpations, which, would inevitably interrupt our connections and correspondence. They too have been deaf to the voice of justice and of consanguinity. We must, therefore, acquiesce in the necessity, which denounces our separation, and hold them, as we hold the rest of mankind, enemies in war, in peace friends.

We, therefore, the representatives of the United States

of America, in General Congress, assembled, appealing to the Supreme Judge of the world for the rectitude of our intentions, do, in the name, and by the authority of the good people of these colonies, solemnly publish and declare, that these united colonies are, and of right ought to be free and independent states; that they are absolved from all allegiance to the British Crown, and that all political connection between them and the state of Great Britain, is and ought to be totally dissolved; and that as free and independent states, they have full power to levy war, conclude peace, contract alliances, establish commerce, and to do all other acts and things which independent states may of right do. And for the support of this declaration, with a firm reliance on the protection of Divine Providence, we mutually pledge to each other our lives, our fortunes and our sacred honor.

About the Author

Richard L. Freitag is a retired Wisconsin businessman who is displeased with the current two-party system of U.S. government. This book is a call to action.

His life philosophy, background, and business career are described in detail in Chapter II of this book.